Words That Manage

The Thesaurus to Help Managers
Relate, Motivate, and Evaluate

Chris Williams

Asher-Gallant Press
Westbury, New York

Library of Congress Cataloging-in-Publication Data

Williams, Chris, 1952-
    Words that manage.

    Includes index.
    1. Industrial management – Terminology.   2. English
language – Business English.   I. Title.
HD30.7.W55   1987   658.3'0014   87-17434

ISBN 0-87280-131-4

Address all editorial inquiries to: Asher-Gallant Press, 60 Shames Drive, Westbury, New York 11590, or call (516) 333-7440. For orders and all other inquiries:
Caddylak Systems, Inc., 201 Montrose Road, Westbury, New York 11590, or call
(516) 333-8221.

This publication is designed to provide accurate and authoritative information in regard to the subject matter covered. It is
sold with the understanding that the publisher is not
engaged in rendering legal, accounting, or other professional
service. If legal advice or other expert assistance is required,
the services of a competent professional person should be
sought.

From a Declaration of Principles jointly adopted by a Committee of the American Bar Association and a Committee of
Publishers.

Printed in the United States of America.

TABLE OF CONTENTS 7146848

Appendix

Introduction

The purpose of *Words That Manage* is really as simple as it is important. This book is intended to help managers at all levels communicate effectively, for effective communication is essential to one's success as a manager—as well as to the successful operation of a company.

When one stops to consider the role that communication truly plays in an organization, it is obvious that the smooth, accurate, and timely transfer of information can strengthen and otherwise enhance a company's operation. On the other hand, an ineffective transfer of information can greatly impede the workings of an organization, whether in obvious ways or in subtle, indirect ways.

If a manager directing a staff of workers miscommunicates directions to a subordinate, the subordinate will often fail to perform as intended. Clear, precise communication can go a very long way in avoiding this problem—and eliminating frustration for a conscientious manager and his or her efficient staff.

Additionally, in order for managers to carry out their own jobs effectively, they must convey their wants, needs, expectations, and opinions not only to subordinates but to co-workers, superiors, and associates both inside and outside the company.

How to Communicate Effectively

The most effective way to convey any message—whether one is trying to relate information, motivate a worker, or evaluate a subordinate's job performance—is to use simple, plain language that expresses a thought clearly and precisely and to present the thought in an orderly and understandable manner.

Of course, before you can do this, you must determine exactly what it is you wish to convey and the most logical way in which to present this information. The importance of this first step in achieving successful communication cannot be overstated. Often it will enable you to spot missing, ambiguous, illogical, and contradictory parts of a message before you deliver it.

Choosing the Right Words. Once you have determined what you want to say and the most logical, comprehensible way in which to present it, you must choose your words. Select them very carefully, knowing that you must use the most fitting words—words that not only convey the right general meaning but also carry the right nuances and implications—if you are to get your point across successfully.

It is surprising how casually many people choose their words—and how misinformed many are about the true meaning of many terms they use. There seems to be a rather widely held notion that a superficial or general understanding of a term will enable one to use it correctly. And, this is just not so.

Unless you have an extraordinary and broad-based knowledge of the meaning of words, it is imperative that you keep an authoritative dictionary handy and consult it frequently if you are to use language properly. While a thesaurus or a similar reference book on language may prove to be an invaluable tool when communicating, it cannot substitute for a dictionary. Use your dictionary often, and look for shades and nuances of meaning that separate one term from another.

When you have narrowed down your choices to two or three seemingly appropriate terms, consider the implications of each. You may very well find important differences. Consider the terms *forthright* and *outspoken*, for example. Both refer to a straightforward approach in which one expresses his or her thoughts directly or forcefully without hesitation or ambiguity. However, while *forthright* implies sincerity, *outspoken* suggests a brusqueness and a lack of consideration for others' feelings.

You might also consider whether one word—or phrase, for that matter—has a more businesslike flavor than another and is therefore more suitable for use on the job. Describing an employee as *loyal* would be more appropriate in a business environment than referring to him as *true-blue*. In the same vein, calling an economy-minded manager *cost-conscious* would be more desirable than labeling him *tight-fisted*, and calling an experienced worker *seasoned* would be more appropriate than describing him as having been *through the mill*.

Get used to looking for the implications that particular words carry. You will quickly see how strong these implications can be, regardless of how subtle or obvious they are. Consider the difference between asking managers "to *discipline* their *subordinates* to meet deadlines" and asking managers "to *instruct*" or "to *ask* their *staff members* to meet deadlines." The former suggests a controlling, authoritarian approach while the latter suggests a more respectful approach that regards employees as being mature, independent agents.

Using the right words can mean soothing someone rather than enflaming him, disarming someone rather than creating defensiveness, and winning someone's cooperation rather than alienating him. Obviously, a manager's choice of words can have important consequences—both for the manager, and for his or her subordinates.

Using Specifics to Communicate Clearly. Generally, the more specific you are when communicating, the greater the chances that you will be understood. Asking a staff member "to complete the weekly production report soon" is quite different than asking "to have the weekly production report written, typed, and photocopied by the following Monday morning for distribution at the weekly, 10 a.m. staff meeting."

Before conveying information, especially when giving instructions or information that must include certain essential details, try using a simple procedure. Ask yourself the following six questions about the subject to be discussed: *what, when, where, who, why,* and *how.* This should help you assemble or begin to assemble the pertinent specific information.

Notice all the important details that have been left out of the following invitation to employees:

"Join your co-workers next Sunday for a picnic at Seaside Park."

Asking the six basic questions would have helped the writer of this communique begin to assemble the essential specific information:

What: a picnic
Who (is invited): all employees of Smith, Jones, and Pickwick and their families
When: Sunday, June 15
Where: Seaside Park
Why: for employees to get to know each other and their families better, to have some fun outdoors, and to cheer the company softball team as they compete in the corporate league finals
How (will everyone get there): busses will be provided for those who do not wish to drive

Had these very basic facts been established, the writer might have asked himself whether he should elaborate on any of these specifics. He might have added this information:

What: a *company-sponsored* picnic
When: Sunday, June 15, *from dawn until dusk*
Where: Seaside Park, *Picnic Area 4*
How (will everyone get there): busses for those not wishing to drive *will leave the company parking lot at 8 a.m. and return there at 6 p.m.*

As a final step the writer should have asked himself whether there might be anything else that would be important, helpful, or of interest to those invited to the picnic. Had he done this, the following invitation might have resulted:

"All employees of Smith, Jones, and Pickwick and their families are invited to attend a company-sponsored picnic on Sunday, June 15, from dawn until dusk, at Seaside Park, Picnic Area 4. Food and equipment for volleyball, tennis, and shuffleboard will be provided. For those not wishing to drive, busses will be provided—they will leave the company parking lot at 8 a.m. and return there at 6 p.m. Come and get to know your co-workers and their families better, have some fun outdoors, and cheer the company softball team as they compete in the corporate league finals.

"Please inform Mary Smith in the personnel department, by May 15, if you and your family plan to attend. She will be happy to answer any questions you have about the picnic."

Another way of being specific when communicating is by presenting concrete examples that illustrate a point, a thought, or an instruction.

Suppose, for a moment, that you were conducting an orientation meeting for a group of new employees and were discussing what qualities and abilities were most valued within the company. Assume that you were discussing flexibility. You could say something general, such as "Flexibility on the job is considered highly important and contributes greatly to the smooth operation of all departments."

Such a statement is so vague, though, that if you asked ten people what it meant to them, you might well get ten different answers. If, however, you were to follow this statement with specific examples of what you mean by flexibility, you would be far more likely to convey what you intend.

You might offer three or four examples such as these:

• A flexible employee would willingly learn new production methods in order to improve product quality.

• A flexible employee would willingly revise complicated schedules that he or she just completed if department priorities were to change suddenly.

• A flexible employee would adapt willingly to procedural changes instituted by a new department manager.

• A flexible employee would not resist a change to newer equipment, even if he or she would have to go through a retraining course as a result.

How This Book Can Help You Communicate

Words That Manage is intended to help managers do three things that will, in turn, help them communicate effectively:

• *Determine what it is that they really wish to convey.* This book of words and phrases cannot do one's thinking or suggest what one might or should convey in a given situation. However, because it includes many descriptions and examples of desirable on-the-job activity and performance, a manager might consult it when he or she wants to express something about an employee's behavior or performance at work. The manager might wish to express to an employee how best to perform a certain job, might wish to motivate the employee, or might wish to comment on the employee's performance. Whatever the case, while this book cannot tell a manager what to convey, it will, hopefully, spark ideas that will help the manager uncover what he or she really wants to say.

• *Find the right words and phrases to express themselves effectively.* Essentially, this is a source book of words and phrases, and examples of on-the-job actions and performance. The general idea in creating this reference was to compile a book of words and phrases that would help a manager who wishes to convey, to someone else on the job, information regarding that person's on-the-job actions, behavior, or performance.

With this in mind, *Words That Manage* was structured to present fifty main entries, each of which covers a quality or a characteristic that is highly desirable and valued within the typical business organization. Each entry includes one or more definitions for the main-entry word, a list of synonyms and related words, phrases that for the most part express actions, practices, behavior, or performance closely related to the main entry word, and lastly, a number of on-the-job examples of the quality or characteristic covered in the entry. In addition, the book contains six appendices and an index to further help the user find the right words to express himself or herself.

• *Generate specific examples that help clarify what they wish to convey.* This reference contains numerous examples of how the main-entry qualities or characteristics can translate into action or performance. Use these examples as they are or alter them according to your particular situation or set of circumstances. Citing examples is an excellent way to clarify what you wish to communicate.

One caution in using the examples: It is possible that an on-the-job example included in this book might be considered less-than-positive, or even negative, at a particular company. For instance, an on-the-job example of "independence" listed here is "exceeds the formal limits of his/her authority to avert serious disputes with major clients/customers." Some companies might very well disapprove of an employee exceeding the "formal limits of his/her authority" under any circumstances. When using the examples in this book—or any other information presented here—take into consideration the specific nature of your company.

A Few Notes on Using This Book. This source book is not a dictionary, and no one should attempt to use it as such. In fact, it should always be used together with an authoritative dictionary. Consult the dictionary often, checking that you understand the meaning of any words you have found in this book and any other words you intend to use. Be sure to look for shades and nuances of meaning, no matter how subtle they might be—even subtle differences can affect your communications significantly.

You should know, when using this book, that the main-entry words may have more definitions than presented in this book. Only those definitions that are particularly relevant in a business setting have been included. Also, when there is more than one definition for a main-entry word, the definitions are separated by a semicolon, whether they differ slightly or significantly.

When to Use This Book. Once you become familiar with the features of this source book, you will probably find numerous opportunities in which to use it. The following represent just a few of the instances when you might choose to consult *Words That Manage*:

• When assigning a new task or job function—to help you convey exactly what results you expect.

• When trying to motivate an employee who you know has far more potential than his work suggests.

• When presenting specific examples that illustrate how you want employees to perform.

• When seeking a way to inspire eager, improved performance from your entire staff.

Some Words of Caution

It is extremely important to point out that what one says to or about an employee—whether verbally or in writing—can have strong legal ramifications. For this reason, it is imperative that, before you express anything to or about an employee, or about his or her job performance, you consult with the person in your company who is responsible for giving guidance on how to convey this type of information. This person might be a company attorney, or a personnel specialist. Seeking this person's guidance and advice is of utmost importance when interacting in any way with an employee, but is even more imperative when you are evaluating an employee's performance. Take the time to seek this guidance and come to a full understanding of what information you may present to or about an employee and how you may present it.

Words That Manage is a source book of words and phrases. In it, no attempt is made to recommend what a person should express in a given situation. In no way is this source book intended to give professional advice. It is not intended to be a guide of any sort and should not be used as such.

WORDS AND PHRASES

To Help Managers
Relate, Motivate, and Evaluate

ACCURATE

Definition	correct and exact, generally as the result of painstaking care

Synonyms and Related Words

right	meticulous
unerring	flawless
without error	complete
precise	perfect

Phrases

is painstakingly correct
is extremely exacting
exerts great effort to be correct
is always right
is never wrong
emphasizes correctness
is inordinately precise
is greatly concerned with precision
strives for perfection
believes that no job should be done if it is done incorrectly
is careful to avoid all errors
checks and double-checks for errors
produces flawless work

Examples of ACCURACY on the Job

keeps precise records
is extremely careful in his/her handling of details
attends to details methodically and meticulously
transfers information from one source to another without error
never makes errors in arithmetic
always verifies computations
never makes grammatical or spelling errors

takes precise and complete phone messages

conveys verbal messages completely and correctly

maintains complete, up-to-date files

his/her work requires no checking

always checks his/her own work carefully

checks and double-checks his/her work

takes complete and correct notes of meetings

writes comprehensive, precisely stated reports

produces flawless reports

never misspells names or terms

maintains complete and reliable personnel records

meticulously prepares purchase orders and requisition forms

enters data into computers/word processors without error

keeps precise appointment schedules

conveys department information clearly and correctly

gives precise, detailed explanations of department/company policies and procedures

communicates schedule changes precisely and completely

always attends to project details methodically and carefully

carries out complicated procedures/projects in a step-by-step manner to avoid error

follows department/company procedures to the letter

reports his/her research findings clearly and correctly

plans and implements projects carefully to avoid costly mistakes

is greatly concerned that subordinates are producing precise, error-free work

rectifies others' errors quickly and fully

methodically follows standard accounting procedures and
    keeps precise accounting records

carries out all assignments exactly as instructed

always does his/her job carefully, correctly, and thoroughly

ALERT

Definitions　highly observant and on the lookout, aware; quick to understand the real importance and consequences of a situation or an occurrence

Synonyms and Related Words

observant	takes notice of
watchful	conscious of
attentive	receptive
on the lookout	perceptive
mindful	able to understand
vigilant	sharp
wary	keen
aware	

Phrases　*Related to Observation and Awareness*

is extremely observant

pays attention to details

routinely watches for/notices problems

tries to anticipate problems before they materialize

strives to uncover difficulties before they reach the crisis stage

is a conscientious troubleshooter

keeps eyes peeled for errors

watches for/notices others' shortcomings

notices/pays strict attention to developing problems

tracks emerging problems

stays rigorously on top of problems

sees/looks for opportunities as well as problems

is always ready to seize an opportunity

watches for the most opportune time to make a move

notices/is always on the lookout for situations that will bring profit or other gain

Related to Perception

is highly perceptive

displays keen perception

is quick to understand underlying implications

quickly perceives consequences

immediately recognizes implications

recognizes the ramifications of a decision/change

can foresee the effects of a decision/change

is quick to perceive opportunity

can recognize potential for gain

immediately understands the potential benefit of a situation

is quick to see the timeliness of a potentially beneficial occurrence

recognizes an opportunity for improvement

Examples of ALERTNESS on the Job

Related to Observation and Awareness

notices/watches for breaches of company policy

notices/is always on the lookout for procedural breakdowns

watches for/notices activities or behavior that will undermine company goals

observes subordinates for shortcomings

notices/watches for morale/attitude problems in subordinates

notices/watches for deteriorating performance by subordinates

recognizes personal conflicts between associates/ subordinates that are disrupting their performance watches for misleading/unclear instructions or procedures

continually observes the production schedule to ensure that commitments to clients/customers will be met

watches for changes in consumer needs that can lead to new product development and a potential increase in profits

is always ready to seize the opportunity to make a sales presentation to a competitor's client/customer

Related to Perception

perceives the consequences of procedural breakdowns

recognizes the long-term effects of deteriorating performance in the department

immediately understands the ramifications of a breach in company policy

is quick to identify opportunities for increased sales to existing customers

immediately understands how a procedural change can lead to increased/decreased productivity

understands how a legislative or governmental change can open up new markets/lead to a decrease in sales

quickly recognizes how changes in the marketplace will affect company sales

AMBITIOUS

Definition   having great desire and determination to achieve a certain goal. An advancement in position, authority, earnings, or reputation is usually the objective

Synonyms and Related Words

eager to achieve   aggressive

intent on advancing   enterprising

aspiring   opportunistic

Phrases

possesses strong ambition

shows great desire to achieve

is single-minded in his/her pursuit of goals

aggressively pursues goals

exerts great effort to meet objectives

is resolved to achieve

is greatly motivated to achieve

works diligently in hopes of advancement

advances objectives of department/company in hopes of getting ahead

is committed to getting ahead/advancing

strives to get ahead

is driven to advance

is determined to move up

strives to improve his/her position

is intent on upgrading his/her standing within the department/company

continually seeks to better his/her reputation

seeks to enhance his/her value to superiors

is intent on increasing his/her authority

persistently seeks greater responsibility

is eager to assume control

takes control whenever possible

Examples of AMBITION on the Job

works excessively hard in order to get ahead within the company/department

volunteers to do extra work in the hopes of advancing within the company/department

comes in early and works late in order to enhance his/her value to superiors

puts tremendous effort into troubleshooting and improving procedures in the department in order to create a positive impression among superiors

undertakes independent projects on his/her own time in order to enhance his/her reputation as a dedicated worker

completes projects before deadline and requests additional assignments in order to enhance his/her reputation as a serious, productive worker

keeps abreast of industry developments through reading and seminars so that he/she may seize new growth opportunities for the company and gain the recognition of senior management

actively participates in professional/industry associations in order to gain industry-wide recognition

undertakes extra projects to enhance his/her value to superiors

asks to lead committees and task forces so that he/she can exercise greater influence over company/department decisions and activities

takes every opportunity to make presentations to senior management in order to gain exposure and professional recognition

strives to impress senior management with cost-saving proposals/ideas to increase productivity continually seeks to better his/her reputation with senior management

constantly strives to advance within the company/department

aggressively seeks promotions/raises

will do whatever work is necessary to advance

aggressively takes responsibility/authority in order to further his/her advancement

is committed to advancing his/her career

ARTICULATE

Definitions	able to express oneself distinctly; able to speak effectively

Synonyms and Related Words

intelligible	clear
understandable	well-spoken
comprehensible	eloquent
fluent	

Phrases

conveys his/her thoughts/ideas clearly

expresses himself/herself clearly and fluently

is easily understood by others

communicates facts and concepts plainly and distinctly

always is able to get the point across

speaks very intelligibly

gives clear and detailed explanations

never gives misleading or unclear explanations/instructions

conveys information clearly and understandably

conveys information accurately

makes others clearly aware of his/her thoughts/ideas/beliefs

comes to the point quickly and smoothly

never digresses or rambles

speaks/communicates effectively

never has to search for words

speaks eloquently

is well-spoken

is an impressive speaker

has an inviting/entertaining manner of speaking

has an excellent command of language

has exceptional speaking/verbal skills

is a relaxed, entertaining speaker

Examples of ARTICULATENESS on the Job

clearly explains company policies and procedures to new employees/co-workers/subordinates

teaches new production techniques in a clear, step-by-step manner

presents ideas to senior management in a clear, comprehensible manner

explains cost-saving techniques so that even nonfinancial personnel can understand them

is able to point out subordinates' shortcomings smoothly, clearly, and sensitively

fluently and clearly voices his/her opinion on important department/company matters

gives clear, detailed summaries of his/her research findings

describes project goals/objectives carefully and thoroughly for subordinates and co-workers

accurately conveys the findings/consensus of any committee/task force on which he/she works

states exactly what he/she expects of subordinates

always gives precise instructions to subordinates

states precisely why he/she objects to particular management decisions

presents project recommendations logically and understandably

never uses vague or obscure language to relate a decision he/she has made

persuasively promotes the company's products/services at sales presentations

makes effective, professional sales pitches

speaks eloquently at company functions

speaks impressively at professional/industry gatherings

speaks persuasively on behalf of the company at governmental hearings

relates company positions to the press smoothly, clearly, and accurately

ASSERTIVE

Definition   characterized by decided, often emphatic, statements and actions

Synonyms and Related Words

decided	self-confident
certain	emphatic
positive	insistent
affirmative	resounding
sure	instrumental
assured	forceful
self-assured	bold
confident	aggressive

Phrases

makes strong assertions

speaks up without hesitation

makes his/her position known

boldly promotes his/her ideas

emphatically proposes ideas

presents suggestions in a decided manner

makes emphatic recommendations

strongly advocates actions that he/she believes will bring improvements

is often insistent

insists on implementing his/her decisions

takes definite action

acts in a decided manner

often takes charge of a situation

believes that action is almost always better than inaction

acts assuredly

often takes the initiative

is often instrumental in making changes/improvements

tackles problems aggressively

demands that others meet their responsibilities

demonstrates confidence in his/her decisions

is not afraid to make a mistake

is not reluctant to ask for assistance when he/she needs it

is unafraid to confront critics

meets critics head-on

forcefully overcomes opposition to his/her ideas

stands up for himself/herself

stands up for his/her ideas and beliefs

Examples of ASSERTIVENESS on the Job

expresses strong, constructive ideas on most company issues

voices his/her opinions on important office matters

routinely states his/her thoughts regarding policy changes

regularly speaks up at meetings

uses meetings with upper management as opportunities to influence policy decisions

routinely takes the floor at committee meetings/task force sessions

gives his/her honest assessment of others' ideas

readily proposes changes in company policies/procedures

makes strong recommendations on how to achieve department/company objectives

informs management of impending problems and advocates a course of action

speaks up when he/she wants to take on a certain assignment/task firmly states what he/she expects of subordinates

insists that subordinates perform efficiently

insists on accuracy and diligence from subordinates

sets department standards

frequently takes charge of the department when the department manager is unavailable

hires additional employees and engages ouside services to carry out projects that he/she is directing

requisitions whatever resources he/she needs to implement programs that he/she is sponsoring

takes action to get projects off the ground

is often instrumental in changing department/company procedures

tackles problems forcefully

pushes projects forward, even when difficulties arise

stands up for management decisions that he/she has made

confronts those who challenge his/her business decisions

actively seeks opportunities to take more authority in the department/company

actively seeks promotions

openly expresses personal goals

CANDID

Definitions   characterized by truthful, sincere, straightforward expression; impartial

Synonyms and Related Words

truthful	frank
honest	free-speaking
open and honest	free-spoken
open	outspoken
direct	objective
straightforward	fair
forthright	unbiased

Phrases   *Related to Truthful, Direct Expression*

says what is on his/her mind

says what he/she really thinks

calls it as he/she sees it

tells it straight

can be counted on to give an honest assessment of a situation

offers his/her honest opinions directly and openly

is never deceptive, evasive, or unclear when expressing his/her thoughts

never couches his/her opinions in vague language

always speaks honestly, sincerely, and freely

speaks openly and constructively

uses candor constructively

speaks frankly in order to improve situations

tempers his/her candor with sensitivity for the feelings of others

has a talent for speaking honestly and directly without offending others can speak frankly without creating resentments

Related to Impartiality

can render impartial appraisals

is capable of making objective assessments

judges situations dispassionately and fairly

can disregard his/her personal feelings in order to make an accurate evaluation

gives equal consideration to all sides of an issue

Examples of CANDOR on the Job

Related to Truthful, Direct Expression

honestly assesses his/her subordinates' performance, praising good performance and suggesting ways to improve bad performance

openly expresses his/her assessment of company weaknesses at management meetings

does not couch his/her opinions of others' ideas in vague language

openly informs production director of repeated customer complaints about the quality and durability of the company's products

openly expresses his/her dissatisfaction with company policies/procedures in order to precipitate changes and improvements

offers constructive criticism and recommendations for improvement to managers who are not controlling their department budgets/schedules

openly expresses his/her desire to take on a particular assignment/task

openly reveals that his/her department has failed to meet its production quota

tries to help other managers perform better by offering frank suggestions for improvement

Related to Impartiality

assesses project recommendations purely on their merits

considers all sides of department disputes objectively and fairly

recommends subordinates for promotions purely on the basis of ability and performance

assigns projects without favoritism

CAPABLE

Definition   having the ability and/or resourcefulness to accomplish an objective

Synonyms and Related Words

able	proficient
competent	adept
apt	qualified
effective	skilled
effectual	skillful
resourceful	

Phrases

can do the job

can get the job done

is extremely competent

successfully meets most challenges

can, in most instances, produce the desired result

can meet the demands of the job

has the resourcefulness necessary to solve most problems

often finds ingenious solutions to problems

has the acumen needed to make shrewd decisions

has outstanding personal qualities that enhance his/her job performance

has the intelligence necessary to perform effectively

is unusually qualified to do his/her job

is extremely adept in his/her area of expertise

has the proficiency necessary to carry out tasks in his/her areas of expertise

is an exceptionally skilled worker

Examples of CAPABILITY on the Job

regularly meets and often exceeds production quotas

uses time and resources efficiently in order to meet project deadlines

meets company's rigid quality-control standards

rectifies fulfillment errors quickly and fully

organizes research reports so that facts and implications can be easily grasped

creates exceptionally innovative advertising programs that regularly increase sales

methodically follows accounting procedures and keeps meticulous records

enters data into computers/word processors with virtually no errors

performs assignments exactly as directed

inspires extraordinary performance from subordinates

effectively negotiates with vendors and purchases goods and services at the lowest possible price

frequently exceeds his/her monthly sales quota

is often able to sign up customers of competitive companies

is quick to recognize and seize new sales opportunities

accomplishes all formally written objectives for the year

offers constructive opinions and innovative ideas at planning meetings

quickly identifies impending problems and takes the action necessary to avert them

assesses project recommendations objectively and accurately

continually monitors and assesses subordinates' work to ensure first-rate, on-time performance

has the skills necessary to carry out his/her work quickly and proficiently is an extremely effective manager

has an even-tempered disposition that enables him/her to manage subordinates firmly but sensitively

has the intelligence and organizational skills necessary to implement projects effectively and on time

CONGENIAL

Definitions pleasant, agreeable; able and willing to interact harmoniously with others, cooperative

Synonyms and Related Words

pleasant	cordial
affable	accommodating
amiable	obliging
good-natured	compatible
friendly	amicable
genial	companionable
kindly	

Phrases

is easy to get along with

gets along exceptionally well with others

has pleasing manners

always acts cordially

always tries to establish a warm rapport

puts others at ease

has a warm and disarming personality

is warm and inviting

is sympathetic

cordially welcomes new members to the group

tries to understand and meet others' needs

shows genuine interest in others

always maintains harmonious relationships

always tries to establish and maintain a friendly rapport with others

values harmonious and cooperative interaction

understands the importance of cooperation

helps others to interact smoothly

promotes cooperation among others

continually fosters a spirit of cooperation in others

encourages others to work toward common goals

gets along exceptionally well with subordinates, co-workers, and superiors

always tries to put subordinates/co-workers at ease

understands the importance of maintaining an open rapport with subordinates/co-workers

always has pleasant/encouraging words for subordinates/co-workers

acts as peacemaker whenever necessary

uses humor to ease tense situations

warmly congratulates subordinates/co-workers on promotions or special accomplishments

shows genuine interest in subordinates/co-workers

shows interest in the personal achievements of subordinates/co-workers

tries to anticipate and accommodate the needs of subordinates/co-workers

cordially welcomes new employees

is first to introduce new employees to their co-workers

helps acquaint new employees with their surroundings

helps familiarize new employees with their work areas

always calls a staff meeting to introduce new employees

always invites new employees to lunch

greets visitors warmly and professionally

properly introduces people and tries to find common interests and experiences is courteous and pleasant to callers

answers the telephone cordially and professionally

welcomes clients and makes them feel at home

puts clients at ease

treats clients kindly/cordially

encourages a cooperative relationship with clients/
suppliers/associates

promotes a cooperative spirit among subordinates/co-
workers

encourages subordinates/co-workers to work toward
common goals

encourages subordinates/co-workers to pull together

CONSISTENT

Definition	steady, characterized by unvarying actions, behavior, feelings, character, beliefs, or values

Synonyms and Related Words

constant	dependable
steadfast	unfailing
unvarying	faithful
unchanging	reliable
undeviating	predictable
uniform	

Phrases

is constant and predictable

is never in the least capricious

always acts/reacts in the same manner

is, by nature, unchanging and reliable

can be counted on to behave in the same way, regardless of the situation or surrounding circumstances

emotionally, is extremely stable

is steadfast in his/her values and beliefs

adheres to unchanging personal values

abides by his/her chosen code of ethics

Examples of CONSISTENCY on the Job

always uses the same analytical approach to decision making

brings the same level-headedness to all on-the-job disputes and conflicts

always approaches problems calmly and logically

can be counted on to offer constructive criticism and suggest viable alternatives

always remains collected in crisis situations

treats all subordinates in the same impartial way

can always be relied upon to give management an objective assessment of upcoming problems

always does his/her job diligently/thoroughly/imaginatively/ intelligently/proficiently/productively/efficiently/carefully/ energetically/methodically

always interacts with co-workers cordially/honestly/openly

always judges subordinates/co-workers on the basis of ability and performance and never shows favoritism

is continually optimistic and forward-looking

always considers possible consequences before choosing a course of action

regularly makes the most appropriate choice

is never disillusioned by setbacks

never requires prodding to get the job done

constantly takes initiative on the job

never leaves an assignment uncompleted

always attends to project details methodically and completely

can be relied upon to conduct exhaustive research before writing reports

always keeps comprehensive and precise records

is continually attentive to customers/clients

is never complacent about breaches of company policy

pays continuous attention to subordinates' performance

always participates fully

constantly works to the best of his/her ability

shows unfailing commitment to his/her job and the company

remains constantly dedicated to the goals of the company

always acts in accord with his/her own high standards

COOPERATIVE

Definitions able and ready to work with others to produce a certain result; helpful and accommodating

Synonyms and Related Words

collaborative	compliant
interactive	obliging
noncompetitive	agreeable
willing to help	

Phrases

is happy to help

is willing to lend a hand

works harmoniously with others

is ready to pull together

is ready to work together toward a common objective

is a team player

complies for the sake of the team

adapts/conforms as necessary to further the common goal

follows instructions to further the work of the group

helps achieve the shared objective in whatever way he/she can

understands/believes in the value of joint effort/shared effort

Examples of COOPERATION on the Job

accepts assignments willingly

never complains about assignments or workload

is quick to offer assistance to co-workers

pitches in whenever necessary to help colleagues meet schedules

fills in for others without complaining

willingly accepts constructive criticism and guidance

will do whatever work is necessary to advance the objectives of the department/company offers to work extra hours in order to relieve production backlogs in his/her department

strives to improve his/her performance in order to meet department/company production quotas

is willing to do tasks he/she dislikes to further company/department projects/goals/objectives

tries to accommodate co-workers' needs in order to further department projects

disregards his/her personal ambition in order to help reach department goals

shares research findings in order to advance projects

openly shares knowledge and resources with others in the company/department

tries to promote a congenial and collaborative work environment

strives to overcome interpersonal tensions and create harmonious work relationships

always promotes a collaborative spirit among associates/co-workers/subordinates

understands what can be achieved by united/collaborative efforts

COST-CONSCIOUS

Definition	not wasteful of money or other resources

Synonyms and Related Words

economical	economy-minded
frugal	budget-conscious
thrifty	economy-oriented
dollar-conscious	

Phrases

never wastes time, money, or other resources
strives to increase operating efficiencies
watches/pays strict attention to the bottom line
is bottom-line oriented
is never extravagant
continually promotes an attitude of frugality
never spends more than is absolutely necessary
seeks the rock-bottom price whenever making a purchase
seeks the lowest possible price for items of equal quality
knows how to keep down costs
watches the pennies
is always on the lookout for spending excesses
watches for cost overruns
understands the importance of containing costs
constantly seeks to contain/reduce expenses
makes cost containment a top priority
defers nonessential expenditures whenever possible

Examples of COST-CONSCIOUSNESS on the Job

never allows subordinates to waste time on the job/make extravagant purchases

sets priorities so that he/she and others in the department can work most efficiently insists that subordinates perform efficiently

proposes labor-saving/time-saving programs whenever feasible

requires price quotations from several vendors before approving the purchase of goods/supplies/services

tries to barter the company's products/services to acquire needed goods/supplies/services in the most cost-effective manner

considers the quality of comparable items while seeking the lowest possible price

consolidates purchases in order to qualify for volume discounts

watches that office supplies are used sparingly

parcels out office supplies as needed

requires employees to sign for supplies/complete a written requisition for supplies

requires employees to reuse supplies such as inter-office distribution envelopes

keeps telephone calls short, particularly long-distance calls, and requires subordinates to do the same

insists that messenger service and overnight delivery service be used only when absolutely necessary

travels "economy" class instead of first class and requires subordinates to do the same

scrutinizes subordinates' expense reports for spending excesses

insists that subscriptions to only the most essential professional publications be paid for by the company

routes professional publications to all appropriate personnel rather than maintaining multiple subscriptions to the same publications

institutes cost-cutting programs whenever projects run over budget

keeps an eye on the departmental budget in order to stem overruns immediately

defers cosmetic maintenance expenditures, such as repainting and recarpeting, and other nonessential expenditures whenever possible

CREATIVE

Definition   able to produce something original, and often ingenious, as the result of imaginative thinking

Synonyms and Related Words

imaginative   inventive

inspired   innovative

ingenious   novel

clever

Phrases   originates novel ideas

forms innovative ideas

is highly original in thought

conceptualizes effective new means and methods

develops intelligent new systems/procedures

originates inventive plans/programs of action for achieving goals/objectives

comes up with effective ways of improving…

conceives of clever, resourceful solutions to problems

is an ingenious troubleshooter

takes an experimental approach to problem solving

conjures up shrewd schemes for competing with/in…

dreams up ingenious ways of promoting…

originates unprecedented management techniques

brings imagination and cleverness to his/her job

tries novel approaches to his/her daily functions

invents/develops ingenious new products/devices

brings imaginative, progressive thinking to new product development

develops unique, futuristic products

anticipates future needs when developing new products

comes up with innovative uses for new technological advances

is an inspired inventor/creator of new products

has a gift for developing original, state-of-the-art devices

contributes intelligent, innovative ideas to the operation of the department/company

presents unique, well-conceived ideas during department/company brainstorming sessions

routinely develops bright new concepts that benefit/advance the company

makes inventive contributions to all employee suggestion programs

constantly thinks of fresh ways to motivate subordinates

develops effective new techniques for orienting and training new personnel

originates innovative ways of improving the efficiency and productivity of subordinates/employees

develops innovative methods of teaching new production techniques to subordinates/employees

thinks of effective new ways of improving production methods in order to meet the company's rigid quality control standards

comes up with new, more efficient ways to use time and resources

thinks up effective new ways of meeting project deadlines

develops ingenious remedies to problems faced in the research and development of new products/services to be offered by the company

continually thinks up clever new ways of identifying and averting problems in the operation of the company

develops intelligent, innovative ways of identifying and eliminating company weaknesses develops effective new ways of organizing and managing the numerous details in the department

conjures up novel sales presentations and promotional programs

creates inventive advertising/marketing programs

envisions the impact of new legislation on the company's annual sales and originates novel changes to the existing marketing program

thinks of imaginative ways to win back lost clients

generates effective new programs to achieve the desired growth in annual company sales

takes an innovative approach to cost-cutting

produces inventive schemes to boost company growth

makes engineering strides that repeatedly benefit the company and ultimately lead to increased sales

conceives of unprecedented new products

uses the latest technological developments/advances in the field in designing new products/formulas/equipment for the company

envisions the future needs and wants of consumers in developing new, state-of-the-art products

has the vision to invent devices/develop products that are well ahead of their time

is known within the company and the industry as an inspired inventor/designer

is gifted at creating new products that win consumer interest and lead to increased company sales

DECISIVE

Definition   able to make firm decisions

Synonyms and   resolute   unswerving
Related Words
                      decided   unwavering

                      definite   staunch

Phrases   decides with certainty

                 makes firm decisions

                 reaches decisions quickly and conclusively

                 sticks to his/her decisions

                 is able to draw definite conclusions

                 never makes ambiguous or obscure decisions

                 always makes distinct, clear-cut determinations

                 decides issues conclusively

                 decides issues without hesitation

                 resolves questions and problems with certainty

                 never doubts or second-guesses his/her conclusions

                 is sure/confident of his/her decisions

                 always has faith in his/her choices

                 is able to make bold decisions and stand firmly behind them

                 shows strong conviction when choosing a course of action

Examples of   decides, without hesitation, what immediate course of
DECISIVENESS   action to take in a crisis situation/an emergency
on the Job
                     firmly decides what procedural changes/capital purchases
                        to make in order to improve productivity in the company/
                        department

                     determines exactly when to offer employees bonus incentives
                        in order to spur productivity

is certain of what changes in personnel policy will revitalize the staff and improve deteriorating performance

quickly decides the merits of requests to increase project funding

quickly determines how best to avoid upcoming scheduling problems

decides precisely where to cut costs when projects have run over budget

evaluates promotion recommendations and decides which, specifically, to grant

settles disputes between/among employees in a decided, authoritative manner

decides when and where to commit additional funding and other resources

decides what immediate actions to take in order to resolve problems/disputes with clients

decides exactly how to redistribute resources in order to meet production/sales quotas

chooses and lays out clear, specific courses of action for subordinates

makes business decisions quickly, intelligently, and confidently

is never influenced by a negative response to his/her decision making

firmly establishes department/company priorities

promptly determines the best marketing strategy when a competing manufacturer launches a new product

selects specific employees for important tasks/assignments

never doubts policy changes he/she makes, regardless of how wide-sweeping they might be

has confidence in all his/her business decisions

DEDICATED

Definition	devoted to a principle, belief, or purpose
Synonyms and Related Words	committed
	loyal
Phrases	is devoted
	is loyal
	believes in the goals/objectives/purposes of...
	is committed to carrying out the principles and purposes of...
	puts the goals/purposes of...before his/her own
	gives of himself/herself
	gives of his/her time and efforts
	goes the extra mile
	supports
	stands behind...
	makes personal sacrifices
Examples of DEDICATION on the Job	is devoted to the goals and objectives of the company
	is deeply concerned with the company's success
	personally identifies with the success of the company
	feels personally responsible for the success or failure of a project
	has made a long-term commitment to the company
	believes in and follows all company policies and procedures
	does not tolerate breaches of company policies or procedures
	puts in extraordinary time and effort to further the goals/objectives of the company
	works hard to contribute to company objectives
	stays at a job until it is finished

often works late to complete assignments

takes work on vacation

works overtime

rarely misses work

is rarely late for work

strives to improve job skills and on-the-job performance for the sake of the company

takes pride in working for the company.

does everything possible to support the company/ department

speaks well of the company to clients, vendors, and co-workers

believes in the quality of the company's products and services

actively participates in employee suggestion programs

eagerly participates in company-sponsored activities

believes in the idea of the company family

is willing to offer personal assistance to other employees for the benefit of the company

makes personal sacrifices for the good of the department/ company

DILIGENT

Definitions   applies oneself thoroughly and persistently; works steadfastly towards goals; shows strong commitment to undertakings

Synonyms and Related Words

persevering	conscientious
persistent	industrious
steadfast	hardworking
thorough	determined
painstaking	committed

Phrases

Related to Thoroughness

shows painstaking/meticulous attention to detail

applies himself/herself thoroughly

gives it his/her all

spares no pains to get the job done

takes pains to do it right

works with intense concentration

is a stickler for accuracy

is exacting

is steadfast in his/her commitment to quality

is determined to achieve the best results

demands excellence from himself/herself

always does his/her best

Related to Persistence, Perseverance, and Follow-up

shows exceptional perseverance

perseveres, even after repeated frustration

demonstrates extraordinary stamina in carrying out tasks

displays impressive "stick-to-it-ness"

is capable of sustained effort

never gives up

settles for nothing short of success

sees tasks through to the end

never leaves a project unfinished

doesn't quit until the job is done

always gets results

always gets the job done

pursues projects to their conclusion

follows through to the end

is uncompromising in his/her pursuit of goals

carries out tasks methodically

pursues objectives methodically

is focused

is never side-tracked

always remains on track

stays tenaciously on course

shows single-mindedness when pursuing a goal/completing
  a task

is never distracted from his/her objective/pursuit of goals

immediately resumes work after interruptions

follows through aggressively

displays extraordinary follow-up ability

follows up persistently

has excellent follow-up skills

Related to Ability to Overcome Obstacles

surmounts obstacles

overcomes setbacks

goes forward despite problems

works through dilemas

overcomes hinderances

forges ahead

forges past obstacles

remains determined despite difficulties

refuses to be disillusioned

overcomes discouragement

overcomes disappointment

proceeds despite criticism

Related to Effort and Energy

expends great effort to complete tasks

works energetically at all jobs

displays exceptional effort

exerts great effort

exerts remarkable energy

is uncommonly energetic

struggles to solve problems

labors strenuously

works hard

is hardworking

is extremely industrious

Related to Commitment

is highly committed to his/her job

is exceptionally dedicated to his/her job

shows unswerving dedication to his/her job

shows unfailing dedication to the task at hand

is resolved to do his/her best

is a serious worker

is devoted to getting results

is determined to realize the goals of the department/
company

**Examples of
DILIGENCE
on the Job**

Related to Thoroughness

attends to details methodically and completely

checks and double-checks his/her facts and figures

conducts exhaustive research and writes comprehensive
reports

painstakingly reads all reports generated by his/her
department

chooses a course of action only after examining and re-
examining all alternatives

never makes a decision until he/she considers every aspect
of the problem and every possible ramification of his/her
decision

maintains complete and exact records

checks his/her work for accuracy and completeness

carries out his/her day-to-day tasks to the best of his/her
ability

Related to Persistence, Perseverance, and Follow-up

can, and does, work long periods of time on the same task/
problem without giving up

recontacts prospective customers, even after being turned
down repeatedly

stays rigorously on top of subordinates until department/
company projects are completed

monitors subordinates' work regularly

constantly improves department/company procedures in an attempt to achieve the greatest possible efficiency level

continually seeks to improve his/her performance

continually seeks to better performance within the department

continually tries to cut department spending

sees all tasks/assignments through to their conclusion

continues working until all project goals are met

keeps returning to a problem until he/she finds a solution

focuses all of his/her attention on important tasks/assignments/projects until they are completed

checks that, once implemented, revised office/department procedures do, in fact, achieve the desired result

continuously checks that subordinates have carried out assignments as instructed

regularly monitors activities on complex projects to make sure every step is completed and every detail attended to

stays in constant communication with suppliers to ensure that production materials are regularly delivered on time

Related to the Ability to Overcome Obstacles

pushes projects firmly ahead, even when deterrents arise

reworks and resubmits project proposals initially turned down by management

finds alternative methods of completing, on time, those assignments that have fallen behind schedule

uses well-researched facts and logical analysis to overcome opposition to his/her ideas/recommendations

revisits prospective customers and presents additional reasons why they should purchase the company's products/services

is never frustrated or discouraged by his/her failure to make a sale

implements management decisions despite criticism/resistance from subordinates

Related to Effort and Energy

works exceptionally hard to meet project deadlines

carries out day-to-day tasks energetically and strives to increase his/her productivity

works quickly and vigorously all day

works hard to outperform others in his/her department

exerts exceptional effort to meet his/her own rigid standards

puts tremendous effort into research reports and project proposals

exerts great effort to prepare comprehensive and persuasive sales presentations

Related to Commitment

often comes in early and works late

carries out extra assignments on his/her own time

willingly works late into the night to meet important deadlines

puts in long hours and works strenuously when the company faces difficulties

works hard to contribute ideas and recommendations that he/she feels will help the company grow

strives to improve his/her performance for the good of the company

believes in and follows company policies and procedures

ENERGETIC

Definition characterized by vigorous activity, particularly physical activity

Synonyms and Related Words

active	on the move
activity-oriented	on the go
vigorous	cracking
dynamic	busy
full of energy	driving
full of vitality	industrious
full of vim	laborious
full of vigor	diligent
high-powered	hard-working
highly charged	physical

Phrases

has a high energy level

never runs out of steam

never seems to tire

never appears weary/fatigued/exhausted

is intensely active

never remains idle

is a high-powered, industrious worker

is constantly busy

takes on numerous tasks

is happy to handle multiple priorities

carries out his/her duties/jobs vigorously and displays a high degree of endurance

works actively toward a desired goal/objective

shows strong, continuous drive

works at a quick/brisk pace

moves rapidly

never shuffles along

is never slow or lethargic

is continually on the go/move

comes in early, stays late, and maintains a high level of
productivity

continually seeks to take on additional work/assignments so
that his/her time is fully utilized

accomplishes large amounts of physical/mental work

makes repeated sales calls to prospective clients without
tiring

participates in successive meetings without tiring

undertakes daily assignments with a high level of energy
and enthusiasm

expresses excitement about company projects and works
vigorously to help complete them

eagerly undertakes projects and begins them immediately
by questioning sources, instituting research, and
implementing plans

actively organizes company-sponsored sports and
recreational activities

actively monitors subordinates' work/decisions

frequently travels to check on distant company operations

thoroughly orients each new employee to company
procedures and personally introduces him/her to
co-workers

conducts non-stop training sessions for new employees

rapidly carries out inspections of company operations

reads proposals immediately and renders decisions
    promptly

works rapidly and often completes assignments before
    deadline

tackles department problems quickly and vigorously

pushes projects swiftly ahead

acts quickly to stem customer dissatisfaction

EXPERIENCED

Definition knowledgeable or skilled as the result of performance or training

Synonyms and Related Words

practiced	polished
seasoned	trained
versed	prepared
accomplished	expert

Phrases

has performed his/her job for years

has practiced his/her occupation/trade extensively

is a seasoned professional/veteran

acquired extensive experience within the industry before assuming his/her current position

is not a novice/rookie

knows all the ins and outs of the job

knows the fine points of the job

is experienced at every function of his/her position

is well-versed in all aspects of his/her job

has had extensive on-the-job training

has an extraordinary employment history

is considered an expert in his/her field

has impeccable/unbeatable credentials

is a skilled and accomplished worker

is well-trained and requires virtually no instruction or supervision

requires no new training to carry out the duties/functions/responsibilities of his/her position

solves most problems quickly and effectively because of past experience with similar difficulties is a seasoned troubleshooter

immediately recognizes a problem as it begins to unfold and knows how to deal with it effectively

maintains his/her composure in problem situations that he/she has encountered before

Examples of EXPERIENCE on the Job

has worked as a financial administrator for twenty years

served six years in progressively responsible editorial roles before assuming his/her current position of managing editor

has graduated from the company's rigorous on-the-job-training program

has an extraordinary background in marketing

knows all the ins and outs of managing a production department

performs all office/department/company procedures from memory

is extremely knowledgeable of standard accounting procedures and governmental accounting regulations

is an extremely skilled manager/administrator

has learned, through years of managing projects, how to maintain the schedule and stay on budget

knows, from experience, how to keep the department running smoothly and productively

has the experience necessary to implement projects smoothly and effectively

gives effective, professional sales presentations as the result of many years of practice

is exceptionally accomplished in product design and is often called upon to teach/train less-experienced designers

is considered an industry expert by other company managers and by colleagues outside the company because of his/her engineering expertise, is often asked to give an opinion on the research findings of others

is a seasoned troubleshooter of production problems

can detect developing morale/attitude problems in subordinates as a result of prior experience managing personnel

is quick to recognize sales opportunities because of his/her extensive past dealings with clients/customers

understands, from past experience, the long-term costs of deteriorating performance among departmental personnel

knows, from experience, how to convey instructions/ procedures clearly and understandably

understands, from experience, the potential effects of breaches in company policy

FARSIGHTED

Definition   able to anticipate future events or developments and their likely implications

Synonyms and Related Words

foresighted	prescient
forward-looking	able to envision
forward-thinking	able to picture
anticipatory	future-oriented
anticipative	visionary

Phrases

looks to the future

is visionary but practical

can often predict/tries to predict future events/developments

can generally anticipate/tries to anticipate future ramifications/implications of current decisions

tries to envision the future of projects/programs while they are still in the planning stage

generally anticipates problems/obstacles before they materialize/reach the crisis stage

can foresee obstacles likely to disrupt long-term plans

strives to anticipate new opportunities

is able to recognize potential future gains/opportunities

tries to predict future events when choosing a course of action

considers possible developments/future events when choosing the best time to act/implement a course of action

considers long-term thinking/planning essential

strives to develop long-term strategies

always takes a long-term approach

understands the importance of establishing long-term goals/objectives looks to the future for new business opportunities

has an ambitious vision of what the company can become

can foresee how changes in consumer needs can lead to new product development and, ultimately, to an increase in the company's market share

bases short-term business decisions on anticipated long-term results

bases project recommendations on future expectations

can perceive the consequences of deteriorating performance within the department/company

sees how breaches in company policies/procedures can inhibit future company growth

can predict when a legislative/governmental change will increase/decrease sales opportunities

anticipates competitors' actions

frequently projects the impact of new competitive products on sales of the company's current products

requires that sales forecasts be based on several potential growth scenarios/several possible sets of circumstances and events

emphasizes long-term planning

establishes three-year and five-year objectives/strategic plans

establishes short-term milestones that lead to long-term objectives

structures compensation and incentive programs to correspond to long-term company objectives

insists that promotable personnel develop/orient potential replacements

emphasizes the development of new products/services that will enable the company to retain its competitive edge in the future is willing to invest time and funds on new product development now in order to realize gains in the future

researches consumer/customer needs in order to plan for future product development

replaces aging plant equipment with durable, state-of-the-art equipment

develops lines of credit with several banks in case funding is needed in the future

FLEXIBLE

Definition able and willing to adapt to new or different circumstances, situations, or ideas

Synonyms and Related Words

adaptable	open to reason
not rigid	open to change
unresistant	yielding
able/willing to bend	willing to give in
able/willing to accept	amenable
able/willing to conform	compromising
reasonable	persuadable
open to suggestion	

Phrases

is capable of change

bends on issues but does not break

is able and willing to change his/her ideas/actions/behavior

is not rigid in his/her thinking

can be convinced/persuaded to change/alter his/her thinking

is not resistant/unyielding/obstinate/adamant/uncompromising/unpersuadable/set in his/her ways

his/her ideas/methods are not set in stone

is willing to bend the rules when appropriate

knows when to bend the rules

is capable of changing with the times

does not resist change

is willing to conform to new circumstances

adapts when conditions change

is willing to go along with new ideas/to accept new ideas

is willing to try new approaches

can be convinced that there is a better/more effective way of accomplishing an objective/a goal

understands and readily acknowledges that there is usually more than one effective way to reach a goal/an objective

is open to constructive suggestions/criticism

frequently adopts the ways of others

is often willing to yield to the requests of others

will adopt others' methods when those methods are proven to be superior

readily gives in for the sake of compromise

frequently relinquishes his/her stand in the spirit of cooperation

Examples of FLEXIBILITY on the Job

is willing to revise complicated, well-planned schedules when department priorities change

can interact casually or formally with colleagues/associates/co-workers, depending on the circumstances/situation

is able to switch his/her attention from one task to another without experiencing a sense of disruption

can adapt to procedural changes instituted by a new department head or another supervisor

can comfortably change his/her work methods when required by a change in company/department procedures

continues to work comfortably and productively when moved to a new work location

adapts well to a change in the work environment

willingly reduces department expenditures when the company institutes an austerity program

is willing to make design changes in existing products in order to meet new governmental regulations

is willing to revise accounting procedures to accommodate new government restrictions/regulations will try new techniques/approaches to further the goals/ objectives of the company/department

tries new, innovative advertising/marketing programs in an attempt to increase sales

adopts new production techniques to increase both productivity and product quality

never resists a change to state-of-the-art equipment/ machinery, even when it will require complete retraining of personnel

willingly changes his/her management techniques when a better way is demonstrated

will try unusual cost-cutting methods, such as bartering, if they appear to be promising

will change the current employee incentive program if it fails to motivate personnel

seriously considers constructive criticism of his/her work and makes changes that he/she feels will improve his/her job performance

is willing to come in early and work late when asked to help other department personnel meet an important deadline

will work weekends when asked to

permits subordinates to leave early for important personal appointments

willingly fills in when the switchboard operator takes a break

will change his/her lunch hour in order to provide continued coverage in the department

is willing to give in, when appropriate, for the sake of smooth department operation

negotiates contract terms in a spirit of give and take

often yields to associates in order to further a spirit of cooperation within the department/company

allows subordinates to hire temporary help when they feel extremely overburdened

HELPFUL

Definition	willing to assist	
Synonyms and Related Words	willing to aid	obliging
	willing to serve	supportive
	accommodating	collaborative
	accommodative	cooperative

Phrases

is happy to help

is eager to lend a hand

is always ready to assist others

pitches in to assist others

willingly provides assistance/aid

always wants to help

readily gives aid to others

provides support to others

helps out/assists whenever he/she can

eases the burden of others

lightens the load of others

Examples of HELPFULNESS on the Job

frequently offers assistance to co-workers

offers to do work for others when they have fallen behind schedule

reschedules his/her work in order to help other department personnel prepare for important presentations/ management meetings/trade shows

volunteers to work overtime to help relieve production backlogs

offers to make travel arrangements for out-of-town colleagues/associates

volunteers to type reports/letters for secretaries who are backlogged is willing to answer phones when the department receptionist takes a break

provides new salespersons with sales leads and background information on prospective clients/customers

explains company policies, procedures, and practices to new employees

takes the time to introduce new employees to their co-workers and to familiarize them with their new work environment

openly shares knowledge and resources with co-workers/associates/colleagues

shares project findings with co-workers/associates/colleagues to help them complete their own projects

shares information about outside suppliers and independent contractors with other managers

offers advice to help co-workers/associates/colleagues meet their job goals

recommends cost-cutting methods that he/she has found effective to managers whose department budgets have been reduced

helps other managers identify and avert impending production problems

contributes his/her thoughts/recommendations on how to increase annual sales and decrease annual expenses

works strenuously and puts in long hours when the company faces serious difficulties

actively participates in employee suggestion programs

helps organize company-sponsored recreational programs for employees

actively participates in professional/industry associations to learn of industry developments that might affect the company

on his/her own time helps lobbying groups that promote company interests

provides prospective clients/customers with whatever information they request that can be made available to them

refers client/customer inquiries to the right department

tries to accommodate a client's/customer's immediate need for the company's products/services

tries to improve a delivery schedule already agreed upon if the customer/client so requests

INDEPENDENT

Definition   able to act on one's own, without direction, help, or
approval from others

Synonyms and   inner-directed   self-reliant
Related Words
             self-directed   self-sufficient

             self-motivated   resourceful

             self-starting   self-assured

             autonomous   self-confident

Phrases   works well without supervision

             carries out tasks on his/her own

             works autonomously

             performs effectively on his/her own

             functions exceptionally well by himself/herself

             prefers to work alone

             feels perfectly comfortable working with minimal
                 supervision

             directs his/her own projects

             implements assignments alone

             schedules and carries out his/her work alone

             carries out routine tasks without being asked

             exercises his/her authority without being told to

             recognizes potential problems and acts to correct them
                 without being asked

             acts on his/her own to overcome obstacles

             solves problems without seeking help from others

             tackles difficulties by himself/herself

             relies on his/her own resources to solve problems

             relies on his/her own abilities to carry out his/her work

decides for himself/herself how best to achieve an objective

acts on his/her own best judgment

makes effective decisions without seeking the opinions of others

decides and acts without seeking outside approval

undertakes projects without input from others

exceeds the formal limits of his/her authority in an emergency/when necessary to avert serious problems/ when necessary to seize an opportunity

assumes authority and responsibility in crisis situations

Examples of INDEPENDENCE on the Job

carries out his/her daily assignments quickly and efficiently alone

works by himself/herself to prepare and organize major sales presentations

makes his/her own business decisions

analyzes production problems and finds solutions on his/her own

conducts exhaustive new product research by himself/ herself

works autonomously, carrying out many department assignments at once

resolves computer problems by working quickly and diligently alone

organizes his/her own presentations and conferences

acts on his/her own to develop sales leads in new markets

follows up on all potential sales opportunities without being asked to

initiates new projects as soon as he/she has completed those previously assigned

anticipates supervisors' needs and takes action on his/her own to meet them initiates preliminary research for a new product he/she feels the company should develop

takes it upon himself/herself to institute cost-cutting measures in the department

takes responsibility for rescheduling department activities when changing conditions dictate it

solves scheduling problems without the help of others

solves personnel problems without calling in others for advice

takes it upon himself/herself to hire additional personnel to carry out department projects efficiently, effectively, and on schedule

assesses and effectively uses promising but unproven methods to solve production problems

never needs the expressed support of superiors in managing and directing his/her department

makes hard business decisions without seeking the approval of others

exceeds the formal limits of his/her authority to avert serious disputes with major clients/customers

goes beyond the stated bounds of his/her authority and responsibility in order to close major sales for the company

INTELLIGENT

Definitions able to reason; mentally alert and perceptive

Synonyms and Related Words

reasoning	sharp
rational	apt
thinking	keen
cerebral	astute
smart	perceptive
clever	discerning
bright	penetrating
ingenious	understanding
alert	insightful
aware	quick-witted
conscious	witty
clear-sighted	

Phrases

possesses exceptional intellect

is a thinking person

is always guided by reason

is an uncommonly rational person

brings uncommon reasoning ability to his/her decision making

considers all possible consequences before choosing a course of action

solves problems through reason

thinks out precisely what steps are necessary to reach a goal/an objective before taking any action

analyzes complex problems in order to find effective and efficient solutions takes a logical approach to troubleshooting/problem solving

is bright and clever

learns quickly

is a smart worker

devises particularly clever ways of reaching goals/objectives

develops ingenious systems and procedures

develops bright new approaches to routine tasks

brings cleverness and a keen eye to his/her job

readily sees opportunities for gain

is alert to problems in the making

is quick to perceive opportunity as well as potential difficulty

is highly perceptive

has a penetrating and perceptive mind

is quick-witted and insightful

brings intelligence and insight to his/her decision making

instantly perceives the probable consequences of a decision/change

understands the potential ramifications of a decision/change

displays keen perception when troubleshooting/solving problems

Examples of INTELLIGENCE on the Job

determines all of the steps necessary to implement a project and the most effective sequence in which to perform them

carefully considers how legislative changes will affect department/company operations

figures out how to use new technological advances to improve the company's products

develops practical, well-considered plans to increase company sales anticipates how changes in the marketplace will affect demand for the company's products and makes well-thought-out recommendations to counter any negative effect

regularly evaluates the company's quality-control procedures and maps out any changes needed to upgrade the company's products/services

conceives of and designs ingenious advertising campaigns

creates intelligent programs to motivate company employees

advances unique ideas on how to stimulate customer demand for the company's products/services

always has astute ideas on how to cut company costs

routinely sees ways to increase company productivity

is always aware of emerging attitude problems among subordinates

is conscious of subordinates' individual needs

is able to recognize unobvious sales opportunities

immediately understands how a recommendation, if implemented, will affect the company in the long run

is quick to perceive how emerging customer dissatisfaction will impact on future sales

perceives the long-term consequences of deteriorating performance in the department

can foresee how offering financial incentives to employees will improve morale and work habits

INTERESTED

Definition	having one's attention or concern aroused and held

Synonyms and Related Words

engaged	involved
absorbed	enthused
occupied	stimulated
engrossed	fascinated
immersed	

Phrases

is engaged in work that piques his/her interest and holds his/her attention

is fully involved in his/her work

is absorbed by his/her work and, as a result, concentrates his/her complete effort on it

focuses his/her complete attention on assignments

cares greatly about his/her work/the company

is highly concerned about the well-being of the company

finds his/her work highly stimulating

shows great enthusiasm for his/her work

Examples of INTEREST on the Job

scrutinizes all reports and reference materials relevent to his/her job

continues to work on company projects after regular work hours

takes copious notes at project planning meetings to help him/her carry out tasks thoroughly and effectively

asks thoughtful, probing questions at project orientation meetings

undertakes independent research to answer questions that he/she encounters in carrying out assignments

seeks out knowledgeable employees or industry experts to help solve problems hindering his/her progress on an assignment cares about the company's progress and growth

is concerned with carrying out company procedures to the letter and abiding by all company policies

is concerned that a team spirit be fostered within the company

finds the research and development of new products fascinating

is stimulated by the challenge of enhancing the company's competitiveness in the industry

KNOWLEDGEABLE

Definition   having information about or an understanding of

Synonyms and Related Words

informed	erudite
well-informed	educated
knowing	well-educated
versed	well-instructed
well-versed	well-trained
learned	experienced
studied	

Phrases

is well-informed

displays extensive knowledge

is exceptionally well-educated

has had comprehensive training/extensive experience

is extremely well-versed in all aspects of his/her job

knows all the fine points of his/her job

keeps abreast of all developments affecting his/her job or the company

takes courses and attends seminars to increase his/her knowledge in his/her area of professional expertise

has, through training and experience, learned a great deal in his/her occupational field

has accumulated a wealth of job-related information through his/her many years of experience

has, through the years, acquired an intimate understanding of his/her job functions

Examples of KNOWLEDGE on the Job

is well-informed about most industry issues

is well-versed on modern management theory

knows of numerous ways to cut department costs

knows which lobbying groups to contact to promote various company interests

knows whom in the industry to turn to for various types of information

knows the fine points of corporate etiquette

is well-acquainted with the research methods generally used by the company's research and development department

has full knowledge and understanding of the company's production procedures

knows the company's procedure for issuing purchase orders and paying invoices

knows the best, most reliable suppliers and outside contractors to engage for routine services

knows the company's procedures for importing products for resale in the U.S.

is familiar with many available software programs relevent to his/her department

knows what features to look for when purchasing new office equipment

is considered the company expert on corporate financial procedures

knows all of the company's customer service guidelines and procedures

keeps abreast of all marketplace developments relevent to the company

has taken numerous accounting and finance courses

studies industry publications to learn of new legislation or government regulations affecting company operations

has participated in seminars on contract negotiation

has taken advanced courses on human resources management

regularly attends industry conferences, seminars, and trade shows

has graduated, with honors, from the company's comprehensive secretarial training program

has maintained an impressive grade point average throughout graduate study

gained an in-depth knowledge of assembly line production methods during an extensive period of on-the-job training

has had long-term experience as a quality-control supervisor

as the result of many years on the job, can spot impending scheduling problems before they materialize

has had the management training necessary to supervise his/her department knowledgeably and effectively

LOGICAL

Definition   able to reason in an orderly way, drawing upon relevant fundamental points to reach or support a conclusion, determination, or solution

Synonyms and Related Words

rational	intellectually sound
reasoning	analytical
intelligent	inferential
thinking	deductive
sensible	

Phrases   thinks in a very orderly and organized way

is an exceptionally rational person

is always guided by reason

is capable of sound reasoning

presents organized, cogent explanations

builds arguments piece by piece, step by step

develops organized and sensible systems and procedures

reaches decisions through deductive reasoning

uses deductive reasoning to solve day-to-day problems

reasons out solutions to complicated problems

breaks down complex problems into manageable components, which he/she then examines in an orderly, intelligent manner

examines all pertinent elements of a problem and their relationship to each other before reaching a conclusion or a determination

thinks out every course of action beforehand to determine the most effective steps to take and the most efficient order in which to take them

determines what action is required now in order to bring about a future result quickly recognizes when a proposed course of action is counterproductive to the overall program

begins projects by identifying major objectives and determining what steps are necessary to reach those objectives

determines the best timing for each step in a project by examining the relationship of that step to other steps

Examples of LOGIC on the Job

schedules his/her appointments so that information needed at later meetings is obtained at earlier meetings

deduces the probable impact of a competitor's new product line on company sales and develops a well-conceived plan to counter any negative effect

develops sensible methods for teaching production techniques to new employees

analyzes a customer's needs and shows, in an organized sales presentation, how the company's products/services can accommodate those needs

presents well-reasoned recommendations on how to achieve company growth objectives

schedules and assigns upcoming department activities in order to determine whether to hire additional, temporary personnel

in preparing research and development reports, presents fundamental issues and salient points in an orderly, comprehensible form

arranges the department vacation schedule in a way that minimizes disruption of the work flow

prepares well-organized instructions that are easily understood and followed

develops practical and workable computer programs after analyzing department/company needs

organizes intelligent filing systems

develops orderly, efficient office/factory floor plans

decides on an appropriate marketing strategy after studying all aspects of potential new markets

analyzes the company's advertising objectives in order to choose an advertising agency that offers the required services

decides what specific employee incentives to offer after considering the results of a company survey on employee needs

adds useful new features to existing company products/services to improve sagging sales

examines every aspect of the production process to discover the reason for a deterioration in the quality of some company products

identifies, examines, and finds ways to rectify areas of contention in disputes with major clients/customers

before beginning development of a program to finance research for new products, identifies major goals and all steps that must be taken to achieve those goals

in planning a complete factory renovation, determines when, exactly, construction on each section will create the least disruption of work

MATURE

Definition   displaying the qualities of an experienced, well-developed adult

Synonyms and Related Words

adult	not impulsive
fully grown	self-controlled
fully developed	deliberate
grown up	stable
experienced	settled
seasoned	sensible
poised	practical
self-assured	realistic
knowledgeable	reasonable
aware	responsible
self-aware	reliable
reality-oriented	dependable

Phrases

Related to Development and Experience
always acts like an adult
never behaves childishly
is intellectually and psychologically mature
is poised and self-assured
possesses sophistication and tact
is seasoned and well-versed

Related to Knowledge and Awareness
understands his/her strengths and weaknesses

recognizes and accepts external—and sometimes arbitrary—limitations

knows the right way to act

understands the importance of behaving and reacting appropriately

knows when to be tactful/discreet

knows when to be compliant and when to be assertive

understands how to put others at ease

realizes that confrontation can lead to alienation

Related to Self-Control and Reason

is never capricious/impulsive/flighty

is not given to hasty or impetuous actions

never makes a scene

is always steadfast and predictable

is calm, patient, and even-tempered

behaves rationally and reasonably

brings much deliberation to decision making/problem solving

changes his/her mind/course of action only after careful consideration

Related to Responsibility

acts responsibly

takes responsibility for all of his/her actions

exercises authority fairly and responsibly

is always reliable and dependable

can be counted on/relied on

always comes through

takes his/her obligations seriously

never reneges on his/her commitments

acts dutifully, even when it means carrying out unpleasant tasks

can be counted on to act in an upstanding way

Examples of MATURITY on the Job

Related to Development and Experience

conducts all business dealings with aplomb developed through years of negotiating

is a seasoned manager who interacts with subordinates in a calm, self-assured way

has well-developed interpersonal skills resulting from many years as a personnel director

is a poised, dignified spokesperson with many years' experience representing the company

Related to Knowledge and Awareness

accepts assignments that he/she can carry out effectively, but speaks up when assignments are beyond his/her capability

recognizes that some co-workers are more suitably skilled for certain tasks than he/she is

knows how to project a sedate, professional image when representing the company

knows the appropriate way to react when a subordinate makes unreasonable demands or tries to initiate a confrontation

understands how to tactfully turn down subordinates' requests for time off/salary increases/promotions/ desirable travel assignments

knows how to put subordinates at ease when evaluating their performance

Related to Self-Control and Reason

never makes important business decisions without giving long and hard thought to all implications and possible consequences

never criticizes a subordinate's actions until the subordinate has had an opportunity to explain them

always behaves with proper professional decorum in the officeplace

calmly intervenes when disputes between co-workers/subordinates threaten to disrupt the orderly operation of the department

Related to Responsibility

is a fair-minded manager who exercises his/her authority impartially and responsibly

can be relied upon to carry out crucial assignments on schedule and to alert his/her supervisor immediately if something jeopardizes his/her on-time performance

takes his/her job very seriously

can be counted on to act with professionalism and integrity when representing the company to potential clients, industry associates, and others outside the company

MOTIVATED

Definition
moved to act or perform, particularly by an incentive One may be self-motivated or motivated by something external

Synonyms and Related Words

moved

inspired

stimulated

impelled

energized

eager

willing

Phrases

is highly motivated

is eager

is easily moved

undertakes tasks willingly

is always ready to take on assignments

is eager to perform well/effectively

wants to produce results

works to the best of his/her ability

exerts great effort

is always absorbed in his/her work

is always engaged in work

devotes himself/herself fully to the task at hand

shows strong interest in all aspects of his/her job

tackles job energetically

works rapidly

carries out work swiftly

pushes himself/herself to produce

accomplishes a large amount of work

is intent on succeeding in whatever he/she undertakes

is achievement-oriented

strives to achieve

sets and achieves goals

is goal-oriented

strives to meet objectives

is ambitious

is self-driven

is self-directed

is self-motivated

takes the initiative whenever possible

is a self-starter

never needs prodding

works independently

**Examples of
MOTIVATION
on the Job**

readily takes direction/instruction and eagerly carries out all assignments

acts quickly on all requests from his/her supervisor

is eager to attend seminars and workshops that will help him/her perform his/her job effectively

is highly interested in all aspects of his/her job and is intent on mastering all functions that he/she regularly undertakes

exerts great effort to meet the company's high production standards while maintaining its frequently demanding schedules

often works late and volunteers to take work home

participates fully in all projects

continually seeks new sales opportunities

tirelessly follows up all sales leads

often completes assignments before deadline and seeks additional work constantly exceeds production quotas

sets ambitious annual objectives and always accomplishes them

establishes his/her own sales goals and works diligently to meet them

sets and meets demanding objectives in the area of new product development

often originates and implements projects on his/her own

takes it upon himself/herself to revise ineffective department procedures

initiates changes to the company's marketing program to improve sales

regularly recommends ways to improve department productivity

OBJECTIVE

Definition   able to consider the facts without being influenced by one's feelings, biases, or unfounded preconceived opinions

Synonyms and Related Words

impartial	dispassionate
candid	neutral
unprejudiced	uninfluenced
unbiased	

Phrases   acts/relies on facts rather than emotion

bases decisions/choices on available information and not on personal feelings or preestablished biases

does not allow personal sentiments or prejudices to influence his/her decision making

judges issues solely on the merits

decides issues impartially

evaluates both the strengths and the weaknesses of all proposals

weighs equally the pros and cons/positives and negatives of all proposals

considers all aspects of a question equally

gives equal consideration to all possible solutions to a problem

considers new ideas without being influenced by preconceived prejudices

reviews recommendations/suggestions dispassionately

Examples of OBJECTIVITY on the Job   considers the pros and cons of new financing methods without being influenced by old-fashioned ideas

considers the skills and talents of subordinates when assigning projects and never allows himself/herself to show favoritism evaluates all project recommendations solely on the merits

considers all sides of disputes among subordinates and acts impartially and fairly to end them

bases promotion recommendations solely on ability and performance

gives choice travel assignments to subordinates who are most capable of carrying them out effectively

considers all advantages and disadvantages of a computerized accounting system before deciding whether to adopt one

gives equal consideration to all customer-research findings before deciding what changes to make in the company's marketing strategy

does not allow himself/herself to be swayed by personal feelings when evaluating the performance of subordinates

OBSERVANT

Definitions	watchful; mentally alert, quick to notice

Synonyms and Related Words

watchful	mindful
attentive	vigilant
alert	aware
on the lookout	conscious of

Phrases

is highly observant

is extremely watchful

pays close attention to...

keeps his/her eyes on...

keeps his/her eyes peeled

keeps an eye open for...

watches for...

is on the lookout for...

is always alert to...

takes notice of...

is quick to see

regularly watches for/is quick to see emerging difficulties

notices/pays close attention to developing problems

is always on the lookout for errors

pays attention to details

looks for/sees opportunity

watches for/recognizes the most opportune time to act

notices all significant occurrences in his/her immediate surroundings

pays strict attention to/sees what is happening around him/her

Examples of OBSERVATION on the Job

watches for/notices the very first signs of customer dissatisfaction

looks for/is the first one to see breakdowns in department/company procedures

watches for/notices behavior or actions that, if allowed to continue, would undermine the progress/efficient operation of the department

keeps his/her eyes peeled for/always notices safety hazards in the office/plant

keeps an eye open for/quickly recognizes morale/attitude problems in subordinates

watches for and tries to anticipate upcoming cash flow difficulties

keeps an eye peeled for/is the first to notice violations of the company's rigid quality control procedures

immediately notices when his/her subordinates behave/act unprofessionally or fail to maintain proper office decorum

recognizes when policies/procedures are no longer effective

immediately recognizes when contract negotiations are beginning to break down

is always on the lookout for/is quick to recognize promising new business opportunities

is constantly alert to possible cost-saving opportunities

watches for the chance to sign up a customer/client of a competitive company

always looks for the best time to change production procedures

continually looks for new sources of project funding

is alert and open to potentially effective marketing strategies developed by subordinates/co-workers

is continually aware of what is going on in his/her department pays close attention to the operation of the department/company

notices increasing disorderliness in the work areas

sees when the day-to-day operations begin to suffer because of tardiness, absenteeism, or a lack of motivation among employees

watches for/always notices promising performance by department personnel

ORGANIZED

Definition
able to systematically arrange items, details, functions, or other elements in a logical, integrated manner

Synonyms and Related Words

systematic	well-ordered
methodical	well-structured
orderly	well-arranged
planned	coordinated
well-planned	integrated

Phrases

thinks in a very orderly way

organizes his/her thoughts logically

often uses deductive reasoning to solve problems or reach decisions

tries to establish cause-effect relationships when troubleshooting

presents organized, well-reasoned explanations

builds arguments logically, step by step

structures reports so that the important points are presented in the most comprehensible manner

categorizes items and arranges them in orderly groupings

keeps an orderly, efficiently arranged work area

carries out tasks methodically

insists that subordinates work methodically

develops well-structured procedures and systems

develops work systems in which functions are integrated and coordinated

after identifying all activities necessary to accomplish a certain objective, determines the most logical, efficient order in which to carry out those activities

Examples of ORGANIZATION on the Job

brings an orderly thought process and a methodical work style to his/her position as a computer programmer

often uses deductive reasoning to determine the cause of assembly line problems and other production difficulties

tries to find cause-effect relationships behind decreased department/company productivity

conveys instructions to subordinates in a highly comprehensible step-by-step manner

builds a case for the development of a certain new product by presenting, in order of importance, the potential benefits — for example, increased sales, an increase in the company's market share, enhancement of the company's reputation as a technological leader, and the development of related products that will further advance the company

maintains an orderly, efficiently planned work station where every item is kept in its proper place

arranges tools so that those used most frequently are within the shortest reach

keeps organized, up-to-date office files

plans out daily tasks after determining the most efficient and practical order in which to carry them out

keeps flow charts to measure progress on important projects

keeps detailed schedules, as well as progress charts, for all complex projects/assignments

constructs a graphic representation of all elements of a major project and their interrelationships

plans efficient layouts of office work stations and plant equipment

assembles financial data and other pertinent information, then uses cash flow projection methods to try to anticipate upcoming cash shortages

considers all factors that might affect the company's annual growth, then develops a plan that maximizes all potential opportunity and minimizes the effect of all potential obstacles

examines the features of different financing methods before structuring a program that utilizes as many methods as necessary, in whatever proportions necessary to meet all of the company's needs

PATIENT

Definitions   willing to wait calmly without feeling annoyed, angry, anxious, or otherwise discontented; able to restrain from reacting rashly or ill-temperedly; not given to hurried or rash actions

Synonyms and Related Words

calm	accepting
collected	tolerant
composed	enduring
poised	long-suffering
unexcitable	uncomplaining
imperturbable	unresistant
even-tempered	forbearing
relaxed	unhurried
easy-going	persevering
passive	plodding

Phrases   *Related to Calmness and Composure*

is calm and tolerant with others

does not allow himself/herself to become agitated or disgruntled by the actions or behavior of others

never gets excited when someone tries to provoke him/her

remains unruffled when others behave in an annoying or a disturbing way

remains composed and controlled when others are being difficult

does not allow himself/herself to become annoyed by others' slowness or other shortcomings

does not allow himself/herself to become angry or upset about unfolding events that displease him/her waits calmly for difficult times to pass

calmly bides his/her time until an unpleasant event has
passed

Related to Tolerance and Forbearance

restrains himself/herself from reacting hostily when
provoked

keeps himself/herself under control when he/she is put
under stress or strain

never reacts harshly to others' difficiencies/shortcomings

never acts belligerently when someone assails an idea of
his/hers

objects to unjust barbs with poise and self-control

never reacts nastily when he/she has been kept waiting

reacts philosophically to difficulties/long waits resulting
from others' incompetence

Related to Unhurried Pursuit

pursues goals/objectives in a thorough, persevering,
unhurried manner

never rushes through his/her work or other endeavors

carries out daily tasks carefully and thoroughly without
pressuring himself/herself to complete them unusually
fast

encourages others to work at a pace that is consistent with
thoroughness and accuracy

**Examples of
PATIENCE
on the Job**

Related to Calmness and Composure

interacts calmly and tolerantly with co-workers,
subordinates, and associates

does not allow the complacency or incompetencies of
subordinates to aggravate him/her, but acts appropriately
to rectify these difficiencies

stays calm and even-tempered when a co-worker or a subordinate tries to provoke a certain reaction from him/her

keeps himself/herself from feeling annoyed or anxious when co-workers/subordinates speak or work at an unusually slow pace or display other shortcomings

does not get annoyed when a new employee takes somewhat longer than usual to learn the functions of his/her position

calmly bides his/her time when the company faces financial difficulties that might affect him/her

Related to Tolerance and Forbearance

does not strike back offensively when a subordinate aggressively confronts him/her

stays collected when his/her manager assigns him/her to a project that will require months of long work hours and the completion of many grueling tasks

never expresses dissatisfaction at a subordinate's inherent inabilities or unavoidable shortcomings

calmly listens when another manager criticizes his/her suggestions or recommendations

retains his/her composure when a colleague's tardiness keeps him/her waiting or keeps a meeting from beginning

Related to Unhurried Pursuits

carries out accounting/bookkeeping procedures in a thorough, unhurried manner to ensure accuracy and completeness

reads reports carefully in order to gather the fine points

carries out research in a slow, careful, methodical manner

PERSUASIVE

Definition   able, through the use of reason or by urging, to cause one to adopt a position, accept a belief, or take an action

Synonyms and Related Words

convincing   impressive

moving   influential

able to induce

Phrases

is able to convince/move/influence others

can elicit a certain response

effectively sways others to his/her cause

is able to change others' beliefs and positions

is often able to overcome others' skepticism or indifference

moves others to action

can convince others to change their behavior/practices/ habits

has a charming, influential way

wins over others with wit and charm

has a pleasing, engaging, and influential presence

uses a disarming, well-reasoned approach to win others to his/her cause

builds impressive arguments

gives convincing explanations

uses logic and reason to build a case

influences others' positions and beliefs by presenting intelligent, well-reasoned arguments

makes his/her points convincingly

is almost always able to "sell" his/her position

makes stirring requests of others

makes earnest appeals

implores others to follow his/her lead

makes strong, genuine pleas that receive a wide positive response

Examples of PERSUASION on the Job

often sways other managers to his/her position at staff meetings

effectively promotes the company's products/services

points out a department's weaknesses diplomatically and constructively so that the department manager will accept recommendations for improvement without feeling threatened or severely criticized

speaks convincingly of the company's financial promise and bright future at meetings of prospective investors

at government environmental hearings, firmly conveys the company's strong commitment to protecting the environment

frequently talks subordinates into correcting bad work habits

uses his/her engaging presence and forward-looking optimism to get subordinates firmly behind a new project

convincingly argues in favor of new product proposals before the executive planning committee

presents well-researched facts and sound extrapolations when recommending effective ways to reach company goals

handily "sells" the marketing director on innovative new advertising programs by documenting expected sales results

uses logic and well-researched facts to overcome opposition to increasing the annual budget for new product development

convinces the office manager to upgrade the office environment by citing expected benefits such as increased employee comfort and motivation and an improved company image for visitors

approaches employees earnestly when explaining why they must work evenings and Saturdays if the department is to meet an imperative deadline

makes sincere appeals to employees when the company needs to increase productivity in order to improve a weak financial picture

can stir a poorly performing employee to make a personal commitment to improve his/her work

POSITIVE

Definition   tending to accept rather than reject, approve rather than disapprove, agree rather than disagree, and promote rather than impede

Synonyms and Related Words

accepting	assenting
approving	concurring
supportive	affirming
encouraging	affirmative
optimistic	constructive
agreeing	progressive

Phrases

tends to say "yes" rather than "no"

tends to allow rather than prohibit

tends to support rather than condemn

tends to encourage rather than hinder

almost always approves plans to move forward

encourages others to take action to advance their goals/ objectives

greets others' ideas with enthusiasm rather than skepticism

takes an optimistic view of the future/future prospects

focuses on potential gains rather than potential losses

concentrates on the good elements of a plan/a proposal/an idea rather than the bad elements

sees the half-filled glass as being half full, not half empty

displays and promotes a "can do" attitude

tries to improve ideas/plans/proposals rather than rejecting them outright

tries to further activities rather than curtailing or impeding them believes in building up rather than tearing down

chooses forward movement over standing still

gets behind progressive ideas

always supports progress

never opposes constructive proposals

fosters a progressive, forward-looking spirit in others

Examples of POSITIVENESS on the Job

approves well-conceived proposals to expand and upgrade the company's trade show exhibits

approves the purchase of state-of-the-art equipment to increase future efficiency and productivity

supports changing the company's employee incentive program when the existing program no longer succeeds in motivating employees

approves subordinates' requests whenever possible and appropriate

encourages new employees to ask questions at orientation meetings and training sessions

encourages the development of innovative ways to uncover new sales opportunities

supports new employees instead of condemning them when they take an inordinately long time to learn their new job functions

encourages subordinates to make suggestions and recommendations on how to further company growth or otherwise advance the company

encourages subordinates to take action to reach their personal work goals within the company

is very optimistic about the company's future progress and growth

sees a bright financial future for the company

focuses on the potential gain from the development of a new product, not the possible loss

when considering whether to change to a computerized accounting system, concentrates on the ultimate advantages and not the temporary inconveniences that would accompany a changeover

when faced with a lack of funds for new product development, seeks out prospective investors and enthusiastically describes the strengths and bright future prospects of the company

evaluates innovative product designs without dwelling on the unlikely possibility of consumer rejection

never rejects subordinates' proposals outright without trying to find some strengths on which to build a new or revised proposal

conducts contract negotiations with confidence and an interest in moving forward

always agrees to try promising new marketing ideas that are likely to increase the company's future market share

always gets behind constructive proposals to advance company growth

PRACTICAL

Definitions useful; having to do with actual practice rather than theory

Synonyms and Related Words

usable	pragmatic
utilitarian	sensible
serviceable	realistic
workable	down-to-earth

Phrases

is realistic and pragmatic

is sensible and down-to-earth

is a pragmatic and expeditious worker

gets the job done efficiently

looks for the quickest, most effective way of getting the job done

employs simple, proven methods/techniques

seeks workable solutions to problems

tackles problems pragmatically

makes sensible, down-to-earth decisions

brings a utilitarian approach to his/her decision making

Examples of PRACTICALITY on the Job

carries out tasks/assignments pragmatically and expeditiously

maintains a down-to-earth rapport/relationship with subordinates

develops workable computer programs after analyzing department needs

uses simple, clear flow charts to monitor progress on projects

develops simple, straightforward policies and procedures

chooses simple, proven production methods

is eager to solve day-to-day problems as quickly and pragmatically as possible

examines the nuts and bolts of a system when troubleshooting

seeks the most effective, cost-efficient solutions to quality-control problems

makes sensible cost-cutting recommendations

realistically assesses the advantages and disadvantages of recommended financing methods

PRINCIPLED

Definition   devoted to high ethical standards

Synonyms and Related Words

high-principled	scrupulous
ethical	proper
moral	decent
upright	honorable
upstanding	reputable

Phrases   has high personal and professional standards

adheres to a strict moral code, which is evident in all of his/her personal and business dealings

follows a rigorous code of conduct/ethics

is greatly committed to his/her personal values

is proper and upstanding

strives to be honest, open, and fair

is open and aboveboard

displays honesty and integrity

is highly regarded for his/her truthfulness and integrity

is as good as his/her word

always keeps his/her word

has a reputation for honesty and fairness

has a strong sense of fair play

strives to find fair-minded solutions

demands the fair treatment of others

treats others with respect and consideration

is a loyal colleague and worker

can be trusted

keeps confidential information to himself/herself

fulfills all obligations to which he/she has committed himself/herself

can be relied on to fulfill all of his/her responsibilities

can be counted on to keep his/her promises

conducts himself/herself with dignity and self-respect

conducts business with honesty and integrity

negotiates in an honest, straightforward manner

never takes advantage of others' weaknesses or vulnerabilities

never exploits a situation at the expense of others

decides issues on the merits

makes objective, impartial, well-informed decisions

Examples of PRINCIPLE on the Job

makes honest representations and claims when promoting the company's products/services

never falsely inflates sales results to make himself/herself or his/her department look good

never misrepresents the company in order to exploit an opportunity

is always aboveboard with outside suppliers

speaks up when he/she feels a subordinate/co-worker/ associate has been treated unfairly

is highly regarded as an impartial, fair-minded manager

properly credits subordinates/co-workers/associates for their new product ideas/for their recommendations on how to further company growth/for their suggestions on ways to cut department expenses/for their ideas on creating innovative advertising campaigns

never asks others to do his/her work because he/she dislikes a particular task

treats subordinates/co-workers/associates with respect and consideration

except in emergencies, does not intentionally overstep his/her authority

keeps sensitive company information confidential

can be relied on to fulfill all of his/her job responsibilities

works extra hours in order to deliver reports or complete assignments when promised

can be trusted to handle the company's financial transactions honestly and ethically

conducts contract negotiations with honesty, integrity, and a spirit of give and take

abides by all laws and regulations that govern company activity

bases all business decisions on the merits and is not swayed by personal feelings

never shows favoritism when assigning projects/tasks to subordinates

PRODUCTIVE

Definition   accomplishes a great deal of work

Synonyms and   prolific   efficient
Related Words
                      effective   expeditious

Phrases   completes a great deal of work

                      has a high work output

                      is highly prolific

                      turns out a prodigious amount of work

                      never remains idle

                      is continually busy

                      performs tasks/assignments quickly and efficiently

                      carries out his/her job functions energetically and
                          expeditiously

                      never wastes time or energy

                      is an industrious worker with a high rate of production

                      takes on numerous tasks and performs each swiftly and
                          effectively

                      carries out numerous tasks in an unusually short period of
                          time

                      expends great energy to achieve superior results as quickly
                          and as inexpensively as possible

                      spares no effort to get the job done below budget and ahead
                          of schedule

Examples of   comes in early, stays late, and maintains a high work
PRODUCTIVITY   output
on the Job
                      regularly exceeds department production quotas

                      accomplishes prodigious amounts of mental/physical work

                      reads and evaluates a huge number of project proposals
                          each month

answers a large number of customer inquiries each day

frequently exceeds the company's monthly sales quota for salespersons out in the field

effectively performs numerous secretarial tasks each day

makes more successful cold calls than any other salesperson in the company

turns out more electrical assemblies than any other plant worker

creates many new product designs that ultimately meet with success in the marketplace

has a well-earned reputation for uncovering numerous sales leads in new markets

is an excellent negotiator who regularly realizes exceptional gains for the company

is an exceptionally effective production manager who uses advanced technology whenever possible to increase plant productivity

asks for additional assignments so that he/she will stay continually busy

carries out thorough inspections of company installations at an unprecedented rate

is able to cut to the bottom line of most problems and solve them quickly and effectively

expeditiously carries out exhaustive research

uses efficient, labor-saving production methods

carries out his/her bookkeeping duties quickly, thoroughly, and accurately

conducts major sales and promotional presentations on schedule and under budget

PROFESSIONAL

Definitions having the specialized knowledge or training necessary to carry out the activities of a profession; able to carry out the activities of a profession effectively and efficiently; having an understanding of, and acting in accordance with, the principles of conduct or the work standards of a profession

Synonyms and Related Words

knowledgeable	practiced
well-trained	accomplished
well-prepared	businesslike
proficient	effective
adept	effectual
expert	competent
versed	efficient
well-versed	ethical
skilled	principled
skillful	scrupulous
experienced	conscientious
seasoned	

Phrases *Related to Knowledge, Training, and Experience*

has the specialized knowledge required to carry out the functions of his/her profession

is exceptionally knowledgeable in his/her professional field

displays extensive knowledge/is well-informed in his/her professional area

knows all the ins and outs of his/her job

is highly trained/has had comprehensive training

is well-prepared to carry out the activities of his/her profession

is considered, by colleagues and associates, to be an expert in his/her professional field

is a seasoned pro

is a skilled and accomplished worker

is experienced in every aspect of his/her job

has impeccable professional credentials

Related to Effectiveness and Efficiency

is competent and efficient

gets the job done without wasting time or other resources

takes a businesslike approach to his/her work

uses practical, highly efficient work methods

Related to Ethics and Conscientiousness

adheres to the ethical standards of his/her profession

never violates the code of conduct endorsed and followed by the members of his/her profession

meets the work standards of his/her profession

performs all work conscientiously and scrupulously

always succeeds in doing a top-notch job

Examples of PROFESSIONALISM on the Job

Related to Knowledge, Training, and Experience

has full knowledge of accepted accounting procedures and follows them exactly

has a full understanding of the laws and regulations that govern the company's operation and sees to it that his/her subordinates observe them at all times

has had thorough training in the proper application of standard production methods knows all the ins and outs of managing a direct marketing department

is exceptionally accomplished in product design

Related to Effectiveness and Efficiency

carries out all tasks quickly and proficiently

has the organizational and supervisory skills necessary to implement projects effectively and within a short period of time

is an exceptionally effective department manager

wastes no time in finding solutions to production/ management/marketing problems

Related to Ethics and Conscientiousness

never misrepresents the company or its products/services in order to close a sale or exploit another potential opportunity

never divulges confidential company information to which he/she is privy

carries out his/her work carefully and responsibly

is a serious worker who scrupulously attends to all facets of his/her job

PUNCTUAL

Definition on time

Synonyms and prompt
Related Words
well-timed

Phrases always arrives on time/at the appointed time

is consistently on time

never arrives late

is never tardy

never fails to appear at the appointed time

frequently arrives early but never late

keeps to the schedule

pays strict attention to the schedule

always meets recurring deadlines

carries out assignments on time

performs all tasks on time

completes projects right on schedule

Examples of arrives at work by 9 A.M. every day
PUNCTUALITY
on the Job is never late for work/meetings/appointments

is always on time for staff/planning/committee meetings

consistently returns from lunch on time

always returns promptly from work breaks

delivers inter-office mail on schedule

promptly turns in his/her time card at the end of the work
week

closes the company's books on time

files the company's state and federal tax returns on time

promptly refunds customers' money

delivers research reports by the appointed deadline
meets every production deadline
completes sales forecasts on time

QUALITY-ORIENTED

Definitions   motivated to achieve superior results; interested in and appreciative of excellence

Related Words   directed toward excellence

having high standards

Phrases   values quality/excellence

has high standards

shows unfailing commitment to quality

strives to achieve superior results

always strives to give a first-rate performance

takes pride in a job well done

takes pride in his/her workmanship

is an extraordinarily conscientious worker/a stickler for perfection

sees to the last detail in whatever he/she does

maintains high performance standards for himself/herself and others

demands/values first-rate performance and superior achievement by others

puts a high value on others' fine craftsmanship

appreciates well-designed, well-constructed products/ devices

appreciates top-notch/first-rate service

Examples of QUALITY ORIENTATION on the Job   regularly makes recommendations on how to improve the company's products/services

takes the company's rigid quality-control standards and procedures very seriously

insists on acquiring state-of-the-art equipment when necessary to produce top-quality products prepares outstanding sales presentations and distinctive trade show exhibits, which all enhance the company's reputation

closely examines customer complaints in order to uncover areas of deficiency in the company's product design, production, and shipping processes

proposes changes in employee incentive programs when he/she feels that general performance in the company is slipping

always meets the company's rigid production standards

works diligently to meet his/her own high performance/achievement standards

works painstakingly to develop and implement exceptional advertising campaigns that maximize sales and spur company growth

reworks new product designs until he/she achieves an outstanding result

shows painstaking attention to all the details of his/her job

never allows himself/herself or his/her subordinates to perform deficiently, even when workloads are huge and schedules are unusually tight

explains new production techniques carefully and thoroughly so that workers will be able to maintain production of high-grade products

as a quality-control manager/supervisor, is unyielding in his/her demands for exceptional performance and, ultimately, the production of first-rate products

has great regard for subordinates/co-workers/associates who maintain high standards of craftsmanship

chooses products and equipment of superior design and top-quality construction for use on the job

never forsakes quality for price when purchasing products/supplies hires outside contractors if no staff workers are capable of performing a specific job proficiently

recognizes that high-quality services, although more expensive, generally lead to cost-savings in the long run

QUICK-THINKING

Definition able to exercise one's mental powers rapidly, particularly one's powers to comprehend and reason

Synonyms and Related Words

quick-reasoning	quick to react mentally
mentally alert	able to infer quickly
intellectually alert	able to assess quickly
quick-witted	able to judge quickly
sharp	able to decide quickly
quick to comprehend	able to determine quickly
quick to assimilate	able to solve quickly

Phrases

thinks/reasons rapidly

is capable of quick, rational thought

is able to think things out rapidly

has a quick, active/clever mind

is capable of incisive thought

is mentally/intellectually alert

quickly thinks through new facts/data/information

quickly absorbs and comprehends new information

rapidly reaches conclusions

immediately examines and quickly assesses new situations and their likely implications

considers and immediately evaluates new proposals/propositions

quickly assesses and reacts to emergency situations

decides issues swiftly

often makes prompt determinations

can usually solve a problem immediately

Examples of QUICK-THINKING on the Job

quickly considers the pros and cons of newly available financing methods

comes up with creative advertising ideas on the spot

has a quick, clever mind and an extraordinary ability to design innovative new products

can quickly examine marketing objectives and design a multi-faceted program to achieve them

instantly comprehends how a change in legislation or government regulations can open up new markets for company products/services

is quick to perceive new sales opportunities

immediately thinks through and assesses suggested changes in the company's standard production procedures

instantly assesses the probable effects of a raw-material shortage on company production

is quick to assess and react to an office emergency

makes hard business decisions incisively

solves production problems in record time

solves computer problems expeditiously

RELIABLE

Definition able to be counted on

Synonyms and Related Words

dependable	unfailing
trustworthy	conscientious
trusty	responsible
faithful	

Phrases

can be depended upon

always comes through

is, by nature, dependable and constant

can be counted on to behave or react in a consistent way, regardless of the situation or the circumstances

is as good as his/her word

always keeps his/her word

can be counted on to keep his/her promises

never reneges on a commitment

can be counted on to fulfill all of his/her obligations

can be depended on to perform all of his/her duties properly

is faithful and loyal

can be trusted

is trustworthy

can be trusted to act in accord with his/her personal and professional standards

can be trusted to behave in an honest, upstanding manner

is a loyal colleague and worker

Examples of RELIABILITY on the Job

can be depended on to conduct exhaustive research and examine all available information before making important business decisions

can be relied on to project a poised, professional image when representing the company at industry functions or press conferences

can be depended on to cut department spending wherever possible during periods of austerity within the company

can be counted on to promote company interests when interacting with industry associates

can be relied on to stay abreast of technological advances that might improve company productivity, lead to new product designs, or otherwise benefit the company

can be counted on to complete assignments on schedule, even if it means working evenings and weekends

can be counted on to give his/her very best job performance at all times

can be relied on to monitor projects closely and attend to any problems that might jeopardize their timely completion

always keeps his/her commitment to finish a certain job by a certain time

always delivers a job as promised

can be trusted to conduct business with honesty and integrity

can always be trusted to keep sensitive company information confidential

can be trusted to carry out the company's financial transactions honestly and ethically

can be relied on to approach all business decisions objectively and not be influenced by personal feelings or biases

can be relied on to give accurate accounts of his/her department's monthly sales/productivity/expenses

RESERVED

Definition   controlled and sedate, never given to boisterous expression or showy behavior

Synonyms and Related Words

composed	proper
contained	serious
restrained	unobtrusive
dignified	

Phrases

behaves/acts in a controlled way

always remains composed

never makes a scene

always behaves in a calm, even-tempered manner

maintains a sedate, dignified demeanor

always acts/reacts appropriately

is never ostentatious or pretentious

never appears agitated, even when others attempt to provoke him/her

stays quiet and controlled, even in trying situations

carries out his/her duties seriously and professionally

expresses himself/herself quietly but seriously

speaks in a dignified manner

is never loud or boisterous

states even his/her strongest opinions sedately

is never given to excessive emotional expression

Examples of RESERVE on the Job

acts in a poised, dignified manner on the job

maintains proper office decorum

never appears excited or angry, even when a co-worker has tried to provoke him/her interacts calmly and quietly with co-workers, subordinates, and associates

never speaks loudly or acts boisterously on the job

understands the importance of patience and never loses his/her temper with subordinates, co-workers, or associates

RESPONSIBLE

Definition   can be relied on to fulfill one's obligations and
commitments and to conduct oneself in a dependable,
trustworthy manner

Synonyms and   dependable   dutiful
Related Words
reliable   trustworthy

unfailing   faithful

conscientious   trusty

Phrases   is dependable/reliable

can be relied on/counted on

always comes through

takes his/her commitments seriously

never reneges on his/her commitments

can be counted on to carry out his/her promises

can be relied on to fulfill all of his/her obligations

is always ready to answer for/account for his/her decisions/
actions

acts dutifully, no matter how unpleasant a task/job might be

can be relied on to carry out all of his/her duties properly
and conscientiously

performs his/her work scrupulously

can be trusted to work/act in accord with his/her high
professional standards

takes pains to do his/her job correctly and efficiently

applies himself/herself thoroughly

is extremely hardworking

takes it upon himself/herself to correct others' errors

is a serious worker committed to doing the best possible job
that he/she can

is resolved to do his/her very best

shows unfailing dedication to his/her work and to the company

exercises authority in a fair, trustworthy manner

can be trusted to conduct business with honesty and integrity

keeps confidential information to himself/herself

never abuses the privileges of his/her position

is an exceptionally trustworthy employee

Examples of RESPONSIBILITY on the Job

can be counted on to meet the company's rigid quality-control standards

can be relied upon to administer department funds wisely

can be depended upon to keep abreast with changes in the marketplace or new government regulations that might affect company sales

can be relied on to closely examine all sides of an important business issue before making a decision

once he/she has taken on an assignment, sees it through to completion

having committed himself/herself to increasing company sales, will continue to seek new avenues of opportunity until he/she has realized this objective

performs his/her work methodically and meticulously

carries out day-to-day assignments with painstaking accuracy

takes whatever steps are necessary to ensure on-time completion of department projects

takes his/her job seriously and carries it out to the very best of his/her ability

takes courses and attends seminars to keep up-to-date with advances in his/her field of authority

willingly works extra hours to complete assignments/
projects on time

regularly checks that subordinates have carried out
assignments properly

works especially long hours when the company faces
production problems

takes all business decisions very seriously

conducts all company business ethically and professionally

negotiates company contracts with professionalism and
integrity

carries out his/her job functions in accord with the high
standards of his/her profession

carries out the company's financial transactions in an
upstanding, ethical manner

RESPONSIVE

Definition   reacts readily and fittingly

Related Words

quick to react   quick to answer

quick to act   quick to reply

Phrases

responds promptly and willingly

reacts quickly and fittingly

is always alert and ready to respond

can be counted on/relied on to react quickly in any situation that requires prompt action/attention

is always the first to help others

gives a quick reply whenever questioned

answers immediately when questioned

never evades questions/always addresses the real issue

acts immediately on requests/directives

carries out instructions quickly and willingly

gets right to work when he/she receives an assignment

never procrastinates when given an assignment

never puts off assignments

Examples of RESPONSIVENESS on the Job

quickly develops new advertising strategies when market research shows a change in consumer buying patterns

is quick to recognize and take advantage of new sales opportunities

purchases state-of-the-art plant equipment and improves production procedures when upper management decides that productivity must be increased if the company is to regain its price competitiveness in the marketplace

immediately seeks new financing sources when upper management plans new, sizeable capital expenditures freezes funds for nonessential purchases in his/her department when company management announces the institution of a company-wide austerity program

mobilizes his/her department to meet company emergencies

notifies his/her supervisor/manager immediately when he/she observes a dangerous situation developing

notifies the data processing manager immediately when the air conditioning system in the computer area has failed

expedites the shipment of replacement parts to a customer whose equipment has broken down at a critical time

provides prompt, comprehensive answers to questions posed at staff meetings and management conferences

offers full explanations of issues raised by his/her supervisor/manager

quickly rectifies breaches in company procedures when instructed to do so

begins preparing trade show presentations as soon as he/she is directed to

develops comprehensive sales forecasts when instructed to do so

takes immediate steps when asked to develop a program to stem customer dissatisfaction

eagerly begins market research projects just as soon as they are assigned

SELF-CONFIDENT

Definition   sure of oneself and one's abilities

Synonyms and Related Words

certain of oneself	confident
self-assured	assured
secure	unafraid

Phrases   believes in himself/herself and his/her abilities

has a strong self-image

has a high level of self-esteem

is very self-assured

is extremely self-reliant

is sure/certain of his/her abilities

feels very capable in almost all situations

knows that he/she can do most jobs effectively and efficiently

approaches all tasks/assignments with a "can do" attitude

is quick to assure others that he/she has a situation well in hand/under control

expresses his/her thoughts/opinions without doubt, fearfulness, or hesitation

expresses his/her beliefs/opinions with conviction

is always certain of his/her position on an issue

expresses his/her ideas with certainty

is never reluctant/afraid to speak up

presents his/her suggestions/recommendations in a decided manner/with conviction

stands up for his/her ideas and beliefs

speaks with assurance

appears extremely self-assured when addressing an audience

acts assuredly

is not afraid to make a mistake

never second-guesses himself/herself

makes decisions with confidence

is never afraid or reluctant to make decisions

relies on his/her own judgment

trusts his/her own judgment and acts on it without hesitation

takes bold, swift action when necessary to avert or solve problems

approaches problems with a positive attitude

feels secure in difficult/tense situations

is not afraid to confront his/her critics

Examples of SELF-CONFIDENCE on the Job

possesses a strong self-image that enables him/her to manage his/her subordinates effectively

brings strong self-assurance to his/her role as planning director

has unshakable confidence in his/her ability to meet all the demands of his/her job

feels prepared to handle any problem that might arise on the job

feels fully capable of meeting the company's high quality-control standards

regularly volunteers to take on difficult projects

is sure of his/her ability to carry out projects expeditiously and willingly commits himself/herself to tight deadlines

is never reluctant to express his/her thoughts on issues affecting the company

has the self-assurance necessary to react candidly to upper management decisions is always ready to give his/her honest assessment of others' opinions/recommendations/decisions

takes the floor at department/company-wide meetings and confidently expresses his/her thoughts about the issue at hand

at sales conferences, addresses his/her audience with poise and self-assurance

projects a confident and dignified image when speaking to the press

confidently implements innovative advertising programs to spur company sales

makes hard business decisions confidently and implements them without second-guessing himself/herself

decides with certainty how best to solve disputes with important clients/customers

follows his/her instincts when acting to avert impending production problems

implements important business decisions without seeking the approval of others

trusts his/her assessment of most scheduling problems and takes prompt action to remedy them

makes bold recommendations when he/she feels it necessary to solve serious problems in his/her department

exceeds the formal limits of his/her authority when necessary to avert a crisis

will, without hesitation, advocate a strong — and perhaps controversial — course of action when the company faces a serious threat

never allows the possibility of criticism to influence his/her decisions or actions

SERIOUS

Definition   earnestly involved in one's endeavors

Synonyms and Related Words

intent	businesslike
purposeful	devoted
no-nonsense	dedicated

Phrases

is a focused/directed worker

works with intense concentration

is fully involved in his/her work

concentrates all of his/her effort on completing the task at hand

focuses his/her complete attention on his/her work/ assignments

is single-minded when pursuing a goal or carrying out an assignment

applies himself/herself thoroughly

gives it his/her all

spares no pains to get the job done

carries out all of his/her duties conscientiously

performs his/her work scrupulously

considers his/her work very important

takes a no-nonsense approach to his/her work

is never the least bit frivolous or casual about performing his/her duties

never takes his/her responsibilities/obligations lightly

is a devoted, responsible worker

cares greatly about his/her work/the success and well-being of the company

shows unfailing dedication to his/her job

is dedicated to doing the very best that he/she can

Examples of SERIOUSNESS on the Job

concentrates fully and applies himself/herself thoroughly when developing a new product design

carries out daily tasks with painstaking accuracy and attention to detail

conducts exhaustive research before making marketing recommendations

painstakingly verifies all of his/her facts and figures before submitting financial reports to upper management

recognizes the importance of his/her position

never takes contract negotiations and his/her other job functions lightly

is never casual about remedying customer dissatisfaction

as production manager, sees to it that production workers meet the company's rigid quality standards

is devoted to the company's goals and objectives

works strenuously to advance the company's standing and reputation in the industry

is greatly concerned about the company's future progress and growth and works diligently to further both

frequently works late or brings work home

works especially long hours when the company faces financial difficulties

carries out day-to-day tasks to the very best of his/her ability

continually strives to better his/her job performance

SKILLED

Definition able to carry out occupational tasks or techniques proficiently

Synonyms and Related Words

adept	masterful
skillful	deft
proficient	adroit

Phrases

is extremely adept at his/her job

carries out the tasks of his/her job skillfully

demonstrates extraordinary ability and talent on the job

is an extremely proficient worker

has outstanding occupational abilities

has exceptional job/occupational skills

is a well-trained and practiced worker with expert skills

Examples of SKILL on the Job

has the organizational skills necessary to implement complex research and development projects

is an able troubleshooter of production problems

is skillful at solving disputes with customers and suppliers

develops innovative and extremely effective marketing strategies

is adept at handling many priorities simultaneously

repairs plant equipment quickly and skillfully

brings advanced secretarial skills to his/her job

is an able production worker who is extremely deft at most production techniques

is an exceptional salesperson who often wins away customers of competitive companies

is able to assess planning decisions accurately and to anticipate their ultimate ramifications is an extremely effective marketing manager

repeatedly develops innovative and successful direct mail
 advertising campaigns

STABLE

Definitions steady, not changeable or flighty; emotionally sound, well-balanced

Synonyms and Related Words

steady	consistent
steadfast	sound
unchanging	solid
unchangeable	self-controlled
constant	balanced

Phrases *Related to Constancy*

is steady and predictable

behaves in a consistent manner

sticks to his/her decisions

rarely changes his/her mind

never changes his/her mind impulsively

is never in the least capricious

decides to change his/her course of action only after careful consideration

never vacillates once he/she has taken a stand

rarely changes his/her position on an issue

is not given to sudden changes of opinion

never changes direction hastily or impetuously

is unchanging in his/her methodical, conscientious approach to his/her work

can be counted on to deliberate long and hard before making important decisions

always brings reason and serious consideration to his/her decision making

Related to Emotional Balance

behaves rationally and predictably

does not act on emotion but rather on reason

is emotionally well-balanced

always exercises self-control

is always composed and even-tempered

is never moody or mercurial

Examples of STABILITY on the Job

Related to Constancy

as department manager, consistently exercises his/her authority in a professional manner

is a steadying influence in the department/company

as a member of upper management, brings consistency to company policy

rarely changes instructions or assignments that he/she has given to subordinates

once he/she has established department priorities, does not change them unless a change in circumstances requires him/her to

will not advocate a change in the company's long-range plan without an extremely good reason

once he/she has stated an opinion about a serious department/company problem, will not change his/her position without extremely good cause

Related to Emotional Balance

has a strong self-image that allows him/her to manage subordinates in a straightforward, fair, and consistent manner

never loses control of himself/herself in the office

never loses his/her temper, even when someone casts aspersions on him/her or his/her department remains composed and optimistic when business deals he/she has nurtured for months begin to fall through

never reacts angrily when he/she fails to get an assignment he/she has requested

never falls apart, even when faced with great professional disappointment, such as failing to get a long-sought-after promotion

SUPPORTIVE

Definition   helpful, advocative, encouraging

Synonyms and Related Words

supporting	promoting
assisting	endorsing
aiding	reassuring
standing behind	assuring
advancing	inspiring

Phrases

comes to the aid of

assists whenever he/she can

helps others bear problems/difficulties

provides emotional support to others when he/she feels it is needed

gets behind others when he/she feels that they need support

gives support to others when they are feeling vulnerable

stands behind people he/she believes in

acts as an advocate when he/she believes in a person or a cause

promotes others' advancement when he/she feels they deserve it

encourages others when they feel disheartened

tries to bolster others' self-confidence when it flags

corrects others in a positive way, encouraging them to make improvements

encourages others to improve their work rather than berating them for unsatisfactory performance

encourages others to believe in themselves

reinforces others' self-esteem by emphasizing their strengths and achievements expresses confidence in others' abilities

uses an optimistic, upbeat approach when others are feeling discouraged

assures others that they can handle difficult job situations or demands

gets behind others' recommendations when he/she feels that those recommendations will benefit the company

Examples of SUPPORT on the Job

aids co-workers whenever he/she can

whenever the department workload increases dramatically, assumes as much of the burden as he/she can

supports the company during times of financial difficulty by working long hours and by trying to find ways to cut costs

recognizes when a co-worker needs emotional support and comes to his/her aid

helps shoulder co-workers' on-the-job problems when they seem distressed and overwhelmed

provides support to co-workers who feel especially vulnerable or threatened when changes in senior or middle management personnel occur

acts as an advocate when he/she believes in the talents and abilities of a co-worker or in a course of action that he/she feels will benefit the company

promotes a subordinate's advancement if he/she feels that the subordinate has proven his/her abilities and will be able to contribute more to the company in a different, more challenging position

points out a subordinate's eroding job performance in a positive and encouraging way rather than berating him/her

tries to bolster co-workers' self-confidence when they have failed to perform a task adequately or have failed to achieve a goal, despite tremendous effort

frequently expresses confidence in his/her subordinates' abilities in the belief that most workers live up to and often exceed positive expectations of them

is happy to support a co-worker's/subordinate's recommendation/suggestion/proposal when he/she sees its merit and potential benefit to the company

TACTFUL

Definition able to handle people and situations delicately and considerately so that no one is offended, hurt, or embarrassed

Synonyms and Related Words

discreet	sensitive
diplomatic	considerate
delicate	thoughtful

Phrases

handles touchy situations carefully and sensitively to avoid angering those involved

presents advice in an inoffensive and nonthreatening manner

never openly accuses or intentionally offends others

never criticizes others harshly or denounces them publicly

corrects others quietly and gently and never berates them

does not express his/her opinions vehemently, especially if others hold strong opposing views

takes pains to avoid antagonizing others

avoids using language that may spark confrontation or defensiveness

delivers distressful news gently and considerately

avoids using language that might hurt others

is sensitive to the feelings of others and chooses his/her words carefully so that he/she does not hurt anyone

senses when someone may be embarrassed by something he/she has to say and makes his/her point delicately

Examples of TACTFULNESS on the Job

commends the positive aspects of a subordinate's decision when diplomatically explaining why he/she must overrule that decision

when denying credit to a customer with a bad credit history, thanks the customer for his/her patronage and explains that the company will be pleased to fill his/her order if prepayment accompanies it

tries to settle billing disputes with customers/clients by conveying a spirit of compromise and good will

uses a constructive approach when advising the production manager that inadequate quality control is resulting in increased customer complaints

compliments recent achievements by the marketing department before pointing out weaknesses in the department's market research methods

talks to a department manager about recent overruns in the department budget without criticizing him/her severely or threatening him/her

never voices his/her opinions on company matters brusquely or vehemently in order to avoid antagonizing those with strong opposing views

is sensitive to the feelings of an employee who has failed to receive a promotion that he/she sought and explains, delicately and honestly, why he/she was passed over

APPENDIX

APPENDIX A: ANTONYMS AND NEAR ANTONYMS

A true antonym is generally considered to be a word whose meaning is *completely* and *precisely* opposite the meaning of a given word. While most words have very few, if any, true antonyms, they usually have several near antonyms. A word can be considered a *near* antonym if its meaning is, in part, opposite that of a particular word. Such words might be thought of as contrasting in meaning.

Because one must use correct, exact words to convey an idea accurately and effectively, it is recommended that you examine both antonyms and near antonyms when trying to locate a term whose meaning is opposite that of a given word. For this reason, this appendix includes both antonyms and near antonyms for each of the fifty main category words presented in this book.

All antonyms and near antonyms are listed alphabetically. Those antonyms that are the "truest"—that is, the most completely and precisely opposite in meaning—are presented in boldface. Also, some lists in this appendix are separated into two or three parts, each of which, by itself, is arranged alphabetically. In such instances, the main category word has more than one definition, and each part of the antonym/near antonym list corresponds to one of the definitions appearing earlier in this book.

One final note: One must understand the exact meaning of a word—down to its subtlest nuances and implications—in order to use it properly. Therefore, you should consult a dictionary in conjunction with this reference book to learn the precise definition of a word you wish to use.

Antonyms and Near Antonyms

accurate	erroneous			unfathomable
	imprecise			unintelligible
	inaccurate	assertive		equivocal
	incorrect			diffident
	inexact			passive
	mistaken			unaggressive
	wrong			**unassertive**
alert	imperceptive			uncertain
	inobservant			undecided
	oblivious			unemphatic
	off one's guard	candid		evasive
	slow to perceive			indirect
	unaware			reticent
	unmindful			**uncandid**
	unnoticing			biased
	unobservant			partial
	unobserving			prejudiced
	unperceiving			subjective
	unperceptive			
	unwatchful			
ambitious	unaggressive	capable		**incapable**
	unambitious			incompetent
	unaspiring			ineffective
	unenterprising			ineffectual
articulate	**inarticulate**			unable
	incomprehensible			unqualified
	unclear			unskilled
	indistinct			unskillful

congenial	disagreeable			vacillating
	unaccommodating			wavering
	uncongenial	dedicated		uncommitted
	uncooperative			
	unfriendly	diligent		failing to complete
	unpleasant			failing to continue
consistent	capricious			remitting
	changeable			tending to give up
	changing			
	fluctuating			indolent
	inconsistent			slack
	unsteady			unconscientious
	vacillating			unindustrious
	variable	energetic		inactive
	varying			lethargic
cooperative	noncomplying			low on energy
	unaccommodating			low on vigor
	uncooperative			low on vitality
	unhelpful			slack
	unwilling to help			slow
cost-conscious	extravagant			unindustrious
	uneconomical	experienced		**inexperienced**
	wasteful			inexpert
creative	**uncreative**			unaccomplished
	unimaginative			unknowledgeable
	uninspired			unpolished
	uninventive			unpracticed
	unoriginal			unprepared
decisive	ambivalent			unseasoned
	faltering			unskilled
	indecisive			unskillful
	uncertain			untrained
	undecided			unversed

far-sighted	unable to anticipate		**uninterested**
	unable to envision		uninvolved
	short-sighted	**knowledgeable**	inexperienced
flexible	**inflexible**		unacquainted with
	fixed		uneducated
	reluctant		unfamiliar with
	resistant		uninformed
	rigid		uninstructed
	unadaptable		**unknowledgeable**
	unbending		unknowing
	uncompromising		unlearned
helpful	unaccommodating		untrained
	uncooperative		unversed
	unhelpful	**logical**	**illogical**
	unobliging		irrational
	unsupportive		unreasoning
	unwilling to aid	**mature**	childish
	unwilling to assist		**immature**
independent	**dependent**		impractical
	needing direction		impulsive
	needing guidance		inexperienced
	reliant		irresponsible
intelligent	unaware		unaware
	undiscerning		undependable
	unintelligent		unknowledgeable
	unperceptive		unrealistic
	unthinking		unreliable
interested	**disinterested**		unseasoned
	distracted		unsophisticated
	indifferent		unversed
	unengaged		

motivated	uninspired		hurried
	unmotivated		rash
	unmoved	**persuasive**	unable to induce
	unwilling		unconvincing
objective	biased		unimpressive
	colored		unmoving
	partial		**unpersuasive**
	prejudiced	**positive**	disapproving
	subjective		discouraging
observant	inattentive		dissenting
	inobservant		**negative**
	oblivious		pessimistic
	unaware		refusing
	unmindful		rejecting
	unobservant	**practical**	**impractical**
	unobserving		nonrealistic
	unwatchful		**unpractical**
organized	disorderly		unrealistic
	disorganized		unusable
	haphazard		unworkable
	uncoordinated	**principled**	dishonorable
	unmethodical		improper
	unorganized		unethical
	unstructured		**unprincipled**
	unsystematic		unscrupulous
patient	anxious	**productive**	ineffective
	excitable		inefficient
	impatient		**unproductive**
	perturbable		unprolific
	intolerant		
	short-tempered		

professional
- unknowledgeable
- unprepared
- unqualified
- untrained
- amateur
- incompetent
- ineffective
- ineffectual
- inefficient
- inept
- inexpert
- unaccomplished
- unbusinesslike
- inexperienced
- unpracticed
- **unprofessional**
- unseasoned
- unskilled
- unskillful
- unversed
- unconscientious
- unethical
- unprincipled
- **unprofessional**
- unscrupulous

punctual
- late
- tardy
- **unpunctual**

quality-oriented
- careless
- slipshod
- undemanding of excellence
- uninterested in quality

quick-thinking
- not mentally alert
- not intellectually alert
- slow-reasoning
- slow-thinking
- slow to comprehend

reliable
- irresponsible
- unconscientious
- undependable
- unfaithful
- **unreliable**
- untrustworthy

reserved
- boisterous
- loud
- obtrusive
- ostentatious
- showy
- uncontrolled
- undignified
- **unreserved**
- unrestrained

responsible
- careless
- **irresponsible**
- unconscientious
- undependable
- unfaithful
- unreliable
- untrustworthy

responsive
- **unresponsive**

self-confident
- afraid
- diffident

	fearful		unsteady
	insecure		variable
	unassured		emotionally unsound
	uncertain of oneself		unbalanced
	unconfident		**unstable**
	unsure of oneself	**supportive**	discouraging
serious	casual		disheartening
	frivolous		opposing
	light		unhelpful
	unbusinesslike		uninspiring
	unserious	**tactful**	blunt
skilled	unproficient		brash
	unskilled		brusque
	unskillful		inconsiderate
stable	capricious		indelicate
	changeable		indiscreet
	changing		insensitive
	inconsistent		**tactless**
	unpredictable		undiplomatic
	unstable		**untactful**

Appendix B: Verbs for On-the-Job Activities and Functions

This appendix presents thirty-seven verbs that express activities or functions commonly performed on the job. Included with each is a list of several closely related verbs. Some of the words presented here — *accomplish*, for example — represent activities that are rather general in nature. Others, such as *address* and *instruct*, represent more specific activities.

accomplish	carry out		solve
	complete		tabulate
	meet objectives		verify
address	give talks/speeches	**communicate**	work out
	lecture		advise
	present		announce
	speak		apprise
anticipate	envision		convey
	foresee		express
	watch out for		inform
approve	allow		interface
	authorize		relate
arbitrate	intervene		speak
	mediate		tell
	resolve		voice
assist	accommodate	**concentrate**	apply oneself
	help		focus
	offer aid	**create**	come up with
	pitch in		design
calculate	compute		develop
	figure out		devise
			invent

	originate		direct
	think up		monitor
decide	assess		oversee
	conclude		run
	determine		supervise
	judge	**monitor**	observe
delegate	appoint		oversee
	assign		watch
	designate	**motivate**	encourage
evaluate	appraise		excite
	assess		inspire
	judge		move
implement	carry out		stimulate
	execute	**organize**	alphabetize
	put into effect		arrange
initiate	begin		categorize
	take the initiative		coordinate
	take the lead		establish priorities
instruct	demonstrate		file
	educate		systematize
	explain	**participate**	contribute
	guide		get involved
	illustrate		take an active part in
	inform		take part in
	orient	**persuade**	convince
	teach		influence
	train		move
interact	interface		"sell"
	interrelate		sway
manage	administer	**plan**	establish goals
	coordinate		formulate

	outline		exhibit
	schedule		present
	set objectives	**solve**	find the answer
proceed	expedite		troubleshoot
	forge ahead		work out
	go forward	**strive**	attempt
	overcome		endeavor
	push ahead		reach for
produce	assemble		try
	construct	**support**	advance
	generate		advocate
	make		get behind
	perform		promote
	turn out		stand behind
	work	**think/think out**	analyze
recommend	propose		assess
	suggest		consider
relate	articulate		deliberate
	communicate		examine
	convey		infer
	express		reason
	voice	**understand**	comprehend
research	examine		grasp
	explore		perceive
	investigate		recognize
review	examine	**write**	compose
	inspect		copy
	peruse		copywrite
	study		correspond
show	demonstrate		draw up
	display		record
			transcribe

Appendix C: Words That Express Degree

completely

extremely

exceptionally

extraordinarily

exceedingly

remarkably

tremendously

excessively

intensely

inordinately

uncommonly

unusually

especially

highly

quite

very

largely

to a large degree

considerably

on the whole

for the most part

in general

essentially

somewhat

moderately

to some degree

to a small degree

not at all

Appendix D: Words That Express Frequency

always

at all times

without exception

in every instance

invariably

virtually always

almost always

in most instances

constantly

continually

continuously

regularly

routinely

frequently

often

usually

generally

periodically

occasionally

in some instances

from time to time

once in a while

infrequently

seldomly

rarely

very rarely

hardly ever

never

Appendix E: Words That Express Speed or Pace

fast

at a fast pace

quick/quickly

rapid/rapidly

with great speed

swift/swiftly

expeditiously

prompt/promptly

immediately

instantly

reasonably fast

moderately fast

at a moderate pace

unhurriedly

slow/slowly

at a slow pace

sluggish/sluggishly

Appendix F: Words That Express Quality

superior

exemplary

outstanding

extraordinary

excellent

first-rate

first-class

fine

very good

good

good enough

satisfactory

adequate

sufficient

acceptable

average

mediocre

passable

marginal

barely adequate

inadequate

unsatisfactory

not up to par

not good

not good enough

inferior

lacking

substandard

deficient

Index

Titles of keywords are printed in boldface type